The Presence of Grace

and Other Book Reviews by Flannery O'Connor

the presence

Compiled by Leo J. Zuber
Edited with an Introduction
by Carter W. Martin

# of grace

and Other Book Reviews

by Flannery O'Connor

The University of Georgia Press
Athens

Designed by Francisca Vassy
Set in 10 on 12 Trump Medieval type
Printed in the United States of America

The paper in this book meets the guidelines for permanence and durability of the Committee on Production Guidelines for Book Longevity of the Council on Library Resources.

Library of Congress Cataloging in Publication Data

O'Connor, Flannery.
The presence of grace, and other book reviews.

Includes indexes.
1. Books—Reviews. 2. Religion—Book reviews.
3. O'Connor, Flannery—Correspondence. 4. Authors, American—20th century—Correspondence. I. Martin, Carter W. II. Zuber, Leo, 1908–1980. III. Title.
PS3565.C57A6 1983 813'.54 [B] 82–20064
ISBN 0–8203–0663–0

To Jane

I sent you a Bulletin in which it appears I not only review but am reviewed. I am grateful to [the reviewer of my book] as I have a slew of old lady friends, Bulletin readers all, who have been waiting patiently for these many years for me to get enough rope to hang myself with. They never supposed there was a Catholic influence at work in the nasty little stories. This will not change any opinions but will give them pause. I think all you have to do to get the Bulletin sent you forever is breathe in the collection basket on the Sunday they take it up for the Layman's League. I think that Sunday has passed for the year but Fr. McDonough can tell you.

—Letter from Flannery O'Connor
to "A,"* March 10, 1956.

*A woman who corresponded with O'Connor often and at length from 1955 until the author's death. "A," as she is identified by Sally Fitzgerald in *The Habit of Being*, wished to remain anonymous.

contents

introduction

Flannery O'Connor's reputation as a writer first flowered because of her remarkable short stories and novels. To help support herself, she subsequently became a lecturer and was recognized as a lucid, profound critic—straightforward, nonacademic, above cant or jargon, and professedly innocent of theory; her contribution in this role, edited by Sally and Robert Fitzgerald, is published under the title *Mystery and Manners*. When Sally Fitzgerald edited O'Connor's letters and published them under the title *The Habit of Being*, critics and readers immediately recognized that a writer already firmly established as a narrative artist was gifted in yet another form. With the publication of the following book reviews, and pertinent correspondence, we may observe her at work in one more field appropriate to the life of letters.

Her reviewing apparently began in 1956, for on February 19 of that year she wrote to John Lynch, "I have just had the doubtful honor of reviewing *All Manner of Men* for the diocesan paper, yclept the *Bulletin*."* The review probably appeared in the February 18, 1956, issue of *The Bulletin*, but because of the unavailability of a copy of the paper itself, the version published here is taken from O'Connor's typed manuscript, now among her papers in the library of Georgia College in Milledgeville. Subsequently she wrote reviews often and consistently, about twelve a year, until her death

**The Habit of Being* (Farrar, Straus, Giroux, 1979), p. 138.

in 1964, a year in which she published two reviews, the last one being her review of *The Kingdom of God*.

With only a few exceptions, all of her reviews were published in the local diocesan papers. *The Bulletin* had originated as a monthly in 1922 when the state of Georgia was the Diocese of Savannah. In 1954 it began to appear every other week and continued to do so after the creation in 1956 of a separate Diocese of Atlanta. Beginning in 1963 O'Connor reviewed for both *The Georgia Bulletin* (now associated with the Diocese of Atlanta) and *The Southern Cross* (from the Diocese of Savannah). Eileen Hall was the editor of the book page when O'Connor began her contributions. In the summer of 1960 when Mrs. Hall took a job in Florida, outside the diocese of Savannah, the future of the book review section of *The Bulletin* was uncertain. At that time, Leo J. Zuber, a Catholic layman from Atlanta who had been reviewing for *The Bulletin* since 1949, volunteered to take Mrs. Hall's job. O'Connor regretted the loss of Eileen Hall, for the book section, she said in a letter to Mrs. Hall, was "the most intelligent thing they had in the paper, which is pedestrian otherwise. Somebody owes you a big vote of thanks but I doubt if you'll get it" (June 2, 1960). By the next month Leo Zuber had assumed editorship of the page, and O'Connor doubted the success of the change: "A man probably won't have the time or patience to fool with it long, but we shall see" (July 23, 1960).

In the following months and years she became quite pleased at just how wrong she had been. Not only did the page continue, it flourished, and a strong personal friendship between her and Zuber quickly moved from her formal "Mr. Zuber" letters to the familiar "Leo" and visits to Andalusia farm by the entire Zuber family.

This book, indeed, is a lasting objectification of the friendship, for he was in the midst of collecting and arranging these reviews and letters when he died suddenly November 17, 1980. In his characteristic selfless manner, he considered the project a tribute to Flannery O'Connor. It is most certainly also a tribute to him. Zuber's papers were provided by Blanche Zuber, his widow. Sorting through his meticulous work, I came to sense that the project was a work of devotion for him, and I came to understand quite well the remarkable actuality of a life lived within the Church—a trait he shared with O'Connor. His energy was quiet and consistent, unattended by the disingenuousness of intellectual piety or cloying humility; his commitment was an example of the kind found in Flannery O'Connor's fiction most notably by its absence in most of her characters.

The introduction which he began was a personal reminiscence of his first meeting with O'Connor, at Andalusia—an event he later considered symbolic. He remembers how a swarm of bees separated him and his family in their car from O'Connor and her mother. After the bees left and introductions were effected, the visit settled into the engaging rural commonplaces of the O'Connor farm: delivery of cattle, parade of peafowl and geese, and a shared admiration for Georgia's agricultural tabloid, the *Market Bulletin,* from which, she confessed to him, she had gleaned many a character. As for the other *Bulletin* and reviewing, he recalled that she requested books on the Bible and any by or about Teilhard de Chardin.

She chose a broad range of works, reviewing 143 titles in 120 separate reviews between 1956 and 1964. The works were distributed as follows: 50 religious and homiletic, 21 biographies and saints' lives, 19 sermons and theology, 17 fiction, 8 literary criticism, 6 psychology, 6 philosophy and science, 4 history, 4 letters, 4 periodicals, 3 intellectual history and criticism, 1 art criticism. Once she began reviewing, she was quite regular and consistent. Why did she write? Why did she subject herself to the limiting form of the brief review? Why did she publish such work in a local diocesan tabloid where her work would be surrounded by other journalism which she admitted was quite poor and intellectually shallow? At least two answers appear in her lament that "most Catholics don't know what is going on in the church" (Review of *Catholics in Conversation*), and in her recommendation that *Christian Asceticism and Modern Man* "is a choice contribution to Catholic intellectual life." She chose this means, and took it as a charitable duty, to raise the level of Catholic intellectual life by speaking not to theologians, Jesuits, and priests, but to the ordinary layman, to all the Mrs. McIntyres, who (in "The Displaced Person") are embarrassed if Christ becomes part of the conversation.

Like her other work, the book reviews are at one with her religious life. Of course, she addressed her own intellectual life too, in her choice of books such as Charles Journet's *The Meaning of Grace*, which appealed to her in itself but also because it "brings the subject within the grasp of those without theological training." Her purpose and the nature of her forum account for the preponderance of books about religion and theology; in fact, most of the books in all categories are in the last analysis "about religion"—for example, among art criticism and literary criticism are *Painting and Reality, The Metamorphic Tradition in Modern Poetry, Criticism and Censorship, American Classics Reconsidered, The Novelist and the Passion Story, The Victorian Vision, The Image Industries, Christ and Apollo*—all concerned with essentially Christian subjects. Similarly, the seventeen books of fiction were apparently chosen on the basis of their relevance to raising the level of Catholic intellectual life. If the reader is puzzled as to why she reviewed poor novels, the answer is in the reviews: "In fiction there is nothing worse than the combination of slickness and Catholicism" (review of Charles B. Flood's *Tell Me, Stranger*). About *Harry Vernon at Prep*, she complains, "the only 'good' characters are Catholics" and the "heel-hero," though not Catholic "feels a strong attraction to good Catholic living. All this makes a painful book more painful." She objects, too, to a Jesuit's fiction (*God's Frontier*) because the stories fail to "bleed or sizzle." On the other hand, she admires the virtues of good Catholic fiction but refuses to permit her approbation to become unqualified: she acknowledges that *The Devil's Advocate* is an admirable work which nevertheless reached the best-seller list—"a standard of mediocrity through which occasionally a work of merit will slip for reasons unconnected with its quality." But she insists upon the defects as well as the virtues. All of these examples demonstrate clearly that reviewing for her was an obligation, a serious part of her life in the Church—a responsibility which she humorously associates with the cycle of her life as a Christian. She writes to Leo Zuber (November 28, 1961), "Send me any scourgy [*sic*] book you like for my advent penance."

There are some recurrent concerns that emerge as themes in the reviews, and one is to champion freedom of thought among Catholics, as she does in reviewing *Modern Catholic Thinking* (December 24, 1960). She is favorably disposed to changes in Church taste and a liberalizing of repressive Church policies and practices which impede art and the study of the Bible. Nevertheless, she is quite careful about orthodoxy in such matters, as can be seen when she writes to Leo Zuber (July 8, 1962) that she would like to review Teilhard, but on second thought suggests lightly that Zuber send it to a "clerical gentleman" because the Holy Office has issued a warning about Teilhard. Her mention of the Index here is especially clear in meaning, however, when in a review the next month she wishes there were in the Church "a reverse Index which required that certain books be read." Ironically, one of those in question, *The Council, Reform and Reunion*, was by Hans Küng, who has recently been directed by the Vatican to cease teaching in Tübingen because of his questionable orthodoxy.

There is a decided ecumenical spirit in her opinions, too. In commenting on Karl Barth's *Evangelical Theology: An Introduction*, she is pleased to note his contention that theology is after all human work and therefore sinful and imperfect. "This will remind the Catholic of St. Thomas' dying visions of the Summa as all straw. There is little or nothing in this book that the Catholic cannot recognize as his own. In fact, Barth's description of the wonder, concern and commitment of the evangelical theologian could equally well be a description of the wonder, concern and commitment of the ideal Catholic life." On the other hand, her ecumenism is not programmatic one way or the other; she is not reluctant to point out the misfortunes of opinionated Protestant antagonism. In reviewing *The Cardinal Spellman Story* she deplores the *Look* magazine condensation for its emphasis on "an opportunistic individual," whereas "the book itself mitigates this image, and leaves one wondering who produced the condensation and with what malice aforethought" (August 4, 1962). Her fair and sound judgment in such matters is always apparent, as it is in a review of *The Catholic in America,* with which she finds fault on the grounds that "No mention is made of that Catholic parochialism which often incited bitter feelings among non-Catholics" (November 24, 1962).

Comparison of her various considerations of periodicals and journals also reveals her essentially religious commitment in her reviewing. She gives faint praise to *The Georgia Review,* at that time very much a regional quarterly, scoring it for its lack of rigor, its parochialism, and its choice of fiction, which seems to have "travelled much and been rejected many times" (March 2, 1962). In contrast, she is quite generous in praise of the Catholic periodical *Jubilee** because it "extends one's knowledge of the Church and one's pleasure in it"—even while "printing their stories on colored paper of various bilious or harrowing shades of green, blue and yellow" (February 17, 1962).

There are in the reviews occasional moments when not

*See review, February 17, 1962.

simply the religious ideas of O'Connor's fiction are apparent but also the very objectification of them, the concrete reality that characterizes her creation. Speaking of Bruce Vawter's *The Conscience of Israel*, she praises the book for restoring the prophets so that we can see them as their contemporaries did: "In this setting alone it is possible to understand an Isaiah walking naked as a warning to Egypt, an Hosea agonizing over his prostitute wife or an Ezekiel baking his bread over dung to symbolize the destruction to come" (March 17, 1962).

In terms of style, we find in the reviews the same personality so vividly apparent in her lectures and fiction; and we may take this as a great tribute to her, for the unique voice of the artist is one clear sign of genius. Her horse and wagon were most surely not stalled on the tracks when the Dixie Limited was roaring down, and we recognize her as certainly as we know Faulkner, James, Hemingway, Crane, Thoreau, Hawthorne, Melville, or any other great artist.

Her forte is spare precision, as the anonymous *Bulletin* reviewer observes when referring to her contribution to Granville Hicks's *The Living Novel: A Symposium*: "Having the most to say, she says it in the fewest words, which greatly intensifies its impact" (December 21, 1957). Within the limits of space imposed on *Bulletin* reviewers (about two hundred words), O'Connor is remarkable in articulating a great deal. For example, when reviewing two books dealing with Protestantism and the division of the Church, she manages to epitomize Fromm, Barth, Bonhoeffer, Schleiermacher, and Niebuhr, in three sentences containing exactly five independent clauses. In another instance she is the master of the succinct one-liner: "Here are two mediocre biographies of two great men" (October 31, 1963). She can be just as effective with similar brief rhetoric when she approves of a book such as John J. Heaney's *Faith, Reason and the Gospels*: "It is a fine book, not easily exhausted." Similarly, she can pack much critical perception into a few words, as she does in regretting that some reviewers will interpret J. F. Powers's Father Urban as the typical or perhaps atypical American priest: "This reviewer would like to point out that Mr. Powers is a novelist; moreover a comic novelist, moreover the best one we have, and that Father Urban represents Father Urban. If you must look for anyone in him, Reader, look for youself" (November 27, 1963). And her pithiness can be wonderfully objective, as when she contends that "Zen is neither a philosophy nor a theology, but a way of illumination which offers a definite release from the acquisitive values of American society" (unpublished review, 1963).

Even when she approves of the general content of a book, such as *New Men for New Times*, by Beatrice Avalos, she can be withering in exposing its weakness—in this instance, "jargon held dear in educational circles. The rule is: if one word will do, use four; thus 'experience' becomes 'experiential contact with reality.' Bastard words are either borrowed or invented, e.g., 'educand'—an 'educand' is presumably the victim of an educator. A boneyard of dead or abstract or unnecessary phrases is thrown up between the reader and the thought" (March 16, 1963).

One of the pleasures in reading these reviews is such wit and good judgment; another is to savor the quality of Flannery O'Connor's mind at work on the serious intellectual content of her faith. Here is confirmation, if we need it, that her art arose from religious convictions that she subjected to intense scrutiny not only in her heart but in her mind as well.

Editor's Note

Both the published reviews and the manuscripts of unpublished ones contained typographical and lexical errors that O'Connor would have corrected. In a letter to Leo Zuber (August 3, 1962) she complains about them, especially when they alter her meaning, as in *engender* being changed to *endanger* and *gnostic* to *agnostic*. Most corrections of this kind have been made without indication, but in a few instances they are noted in brackets or at the bottom of the page, with an asterisk.

Acknowledgment has already been made to Leo Zuber for his admirable compilation, without which this book would not exist, and to Blanche Zuber for her part in the compilation and her subsequent generosity in making her late husband's papers available. Sally Fitzgerald provided Mr. Zuber with a number of O'Connor letters published here but not in *The Habit of Being*. Professor Marion Montgomery of the University of Georgia and Stanley W. Lindberg, editor of *The Georgia Review*, recognized the value of this project and worked to bring about its completion. Gerald Becham of the Ina Dillard Russell Library, Georgia College, generously provided materials from the O'Connor Collection. And finally Mrs. Regina O'Connor must be thanked for her continued fostering of scholarship relating to her daughter's career as an artist. I am grateful to them all for their help, and I ask their indulgence for mistakes I have permitted to occur in a work of significance to them and to all admirers of Flannery O'Connor.

CARTER W. MARTIN

reviews and letters

1956

All Manner of Men

Edited by Riley Hughes. Kenedy, 1956.

The Bulletin, February 18, 1956 (?)

There are twenty-five stories in this collection, all taken from the Catholic Press. Of this number, perhaps five are excellent. The rest are variously limited in range and depth and generally suggest that they were written in the Catholic college class room. Against that background they are promising stories; in the Catholic Press one might hope for better. In most of the stories, the meaning is not well carried by the characterization; a good deal of piety is portrayed but not always at a depth that would make it acceptable; sin is conspicuous by its absence. Those who do not like to be disturbed by Catholic fiction will be glad to learn that there is nothing in this collection to suggest that the writers represented have been influenced by the writing of Mauriac, Greene, or J. F. Powers. As a whole, the collection says more about the taste of the readers of Catholic magazines than about Catholic writing in this country, for there are Catholic writers still at large who have not been published in the Catholic Press.

It is cheering, however, that none of the stories is tritely commercial and that a great many represent beginning talent which has great possibilities for development. One feels that the editor, Mr. Riley Hughes, having little to choose from, has chosen wisely. In his introduction, he makes the excellent suggestion that Catholic fiction would prosper if were a dozen magazines of the "little magazine" scope and quality, edited on Catholic college campuses or elsewhere. These would be magazines where a high quality of writing would be insisted upon and where it would be understood that to make the effects of the Redemption believable in fiction, the writer needs to set them in a wide range of experience and to feel them at a depth which will often seem dangerous to the peace of popular taste.

The Presence of Grace

J. F. Powers. Doubleday, 1956.

The Bulletin, March 31, 1956

In this collection, Mr. Powers again shows himself to be one of the country's finest story writers. In addition to a deadly accurate eye and ear, he has a sense of form which controls what he sees and hears in such a way that the many levels of meaning which exist in the literal one are all brought successfully to operate in the story. The region which he deals with to greatest effect is the parish, with its heart, the rectory. Here one feels that he has not merely seen the immovable pastor, the ambitious curate, the salesman missionary, the gothic housekeeper, the Regulars of Altar and Rosary, but that he has suffered them and has come through with his Faith intact.

According to Mr. Evelyn Waugh on the book jacket, "Mr. Powers is almost unique in his country as a lay writer who is at ease in the Church; whose whole art, moreover, is everywhere infused and directed by his Faith." Indeed, if it were not directed by his Faith, Mr. Powers would not have been able to survive what his eye and ear have revealed to him, but he is equipped with an inner eye which can discern the good as well as the evil which may lurk behind the surface which to ordinary eyes has long been dead of staleness, so that his work however much directed by his Faith, seems more directed by his charity.

But the explanation for any good writer is first that he knows how to write and that writing is his vocation. This is eminently true of Mr. Powers and it is for this reason that one may be allowed to wonder why in two stories in this collection, he has seen fit to use a cat for the Central Intelligence. The cat in question is admirable, in his way. He has Mr. Powers' wit and sensibility, his Faith and enough of his charity to serve, but he is a cat notwithstanding and in both cases he lowers the tone and restricts the scope of what should otherwise have been a major story. It is the hope of the reviewer that this animal will prove to have only one life left and that some Minneapolis motorist, wishing to serve literature, will dispatch him as soon as possible.

The Malefactors

Caroline Gordon. Harcourt, Brace, 1956.

The Bulletin, March 31, 1956

In a critical essay called "Nature and Grace in Caroline Gordon," Louise Cowan has written that "though the surface of her novels . . . moves toward destruction and despair, the current in their depths moves in a strongly different direction." In her latest novel, "The Malefactors," this current comes openly to the surface and is seen as the sudden emergence of the underground rivers of the mind into the clear spring of grace. The novel's protagonist, a poet who is not producing, is provoked by a recurrent impulse to wonder where his years are bound. After an involvement with a lady intellectual poet, which takes him away from his wife, he comes to the conclusion that they are bound nowhere unless he can return to his wife who, in the meantime and after an attempt at suicide, has found her way to the Church. He comes to the knowledge that it is for him, as Adam, to "interpret the voices Eve hears."

A novel dealing with a conversion is the most difficult the fiction writer can assign himself. Miss Gordon brings a sure knowledge of the craft to bear upon a task that most novelists today would have neither the desire nor the courage to attempt. "The Malefactors" is profoundly Catholic in theme but it is doubtful if it will receive the attention it deserves from the Catholic reader, who is liable to be shocked by the kind of life portrayed in it, or from the reader whose interests are purely secular, for he will regard its outcome as unsound and incredible and look upon it merely as a *roman a clef*. The fact that the conversion is elaborately prepared for and underwritten by the force of Jungian psychology will be overlooked by those who are not willing to accept the reality of supernatural grace. Making grace believable to the contemporary reader is the almost insurmountable problem of the novelist who writes from the standpoint of Christian orthodoxy. "The Malefactors" is undoubtedly the most serious and successful fictional treatment of a conversion by an American writer to date.

The Rosary of Our Lady

Romano Guardini. Kenedy, 1955.

The Bulletin, April 28, 1956

The first most noticeable characteristic of Monsignor Guardini's writing is the total absence of pious cliché. When he considers the doctrine or liturgy or practice of the Church, he rethinks these in the light of modern difficulties and preoccupations. This is often attempted with less success because the attempt is made by one who sees these difficulties and preoccupations as being those of another. With Monsignor Guardini, one feels that these difficulties are his own, that he does not stand on a height above the modern mind coping with its own agonizing problems but infused with grace.

When he turns his attention to the Rosary then, it is not to recommend its daily recitation whole as a cure-all for every spiritual infirmity, but to rediscover how it should be prayed and to relate the mysteries to the growth of Christ in the individual. "The Rosary is not a road, but a place, and it has no goal but a depth. To linger in it has great compensations." It is concerned with Christ as His existence was made possible by the consent of His mother, and Monsignor Guardini shows that it should relate in meditation to the birth and growth of Christ in the person praying as these are made possible by his consent.

He considers that the basis for all exaggerations about Mary is her uniqueness but he feels that these exaggerations are useless and harmful "because the simpler the word expressing a truth, the more tremendous and at the same time the more deeply realized do the facts become." This sums up the effect of his own writing. He proceeds slowly and with a simplicity that reveals a depth of meaning to the reader who is likewise willing to be in no hurry. Monsignor Guardini has written extensively on Dostoevsky and one feels this wealth of cultural background in his spiritual writing.

Two Portraits of St. Thérèse of Lisieux

Étienne Robo. Regnery, 1955.

The Bulletin, May 26, 1956

Those of us who have been repulsed by popular portraits of the life of St. Thérèse of Lisieux and at the same time attracted by her iron will and heroism, which appear even through the most treacly portraits, will be cheered to learn from Father Robo's study that this reaction is not entirely perverse. The author shows that the life of the saint, as it has appeared in various books, has been manipulated in order to make it more edifying. Indeed, he doubts if we may be sure that the manuscript to her autobiography has not likewise been tampered with for the same pious reason. It is by now admitted by Carmel that the saint's photographs have been touched up. Carmel justifies this on the grounds that it is an attempt to achieve a "better average resemblance."

This practice of making the saint appear edifying according to the popular convention of what is edifying is of long standing in hagiography and is based on a different conception of truth from the one we hold now. It is a conception that does not scruple to permit the rearranging of nature in order to make it fit the ideal type; as such, it is more closely related to fiction than to history. That St. Thérèse has been fictionalized by convent sources is now apparent, but Father Robo, in this study, has gone far to uncover the real saint in her very human and terrible greatness, and in this process surely to widen devotion to her.

Many will be loth to part with the legend and particularly loth to part with the face which has so long passed as the face of St. Thérèse. This face, however, is the result of some retouching by the saint's sister, Celine, who was, in the fashion of nuns, a painter. Celine turned the round, comical, fiercely determined face that God apparently gave St. Thérèse into an elongated, sweetly characterless one that she thought did more justice to sanctity. Father Robo, comparing it with untouched photographs, wonders charitably if she did not suffer from astigmatism.

Humble Powers

Three Novelettes by Paul Horgan. Image, 1956.

The Bulletin, June 9, 1956

There is always a loud cry in the land for fiction about people with affirmative values who triumph by the exercise of virtue. Along with the demand goes the implication that none is to be found. Such fiction is indeed rare because it is the most difficult to write, but these three novelettes by Mr. Horgan should prove at least that it can be found, and in this case for 65c. It only remains for those who have been calling for it to assure Mr. Horgan and Image Books a large sale—a highly unlikely possibility.

Virtue can believably triumph only in completely drawn characters and against a background whose roots are recognized to be in original sin. Where there is this knowledge and a knowledge of the Redemption, on the part of both writer and reader, the story can unfold without that strain attendant upon the writer who assumes, and correctly, that he will be read largely by readers who do not share his beliefs. Part of the calm classical quality of Mr. Horgan's stories can possibly be laid to the fact that he seems able to assume an audience which has not lost its belief in Christian doctrine. The rest may be laid to the fact that he is by nature an artist.

In the preface it is noted that none of the stories was written for "the purpose of setting forth as in a tract an exemplary course of behaviour. They were all written because the energetic individuality and empowering belief of their central characters proposed each time an irresistible dramatic pattern. In other words, the story, each time, came first." This is not to say that Mr. Horgan is writer first and Catholic second, but simply that, so far as can be judged from these three stories, he is, as every Catholic writer must be at least in desire, completely both.

Letter to Another *Bulletin* Reviewer, June 16, 1956

If Mrs. Hall sends you any corny books don't hesitate to send them back to her. It will happen until she gets your tastes in mind. She has sent me a couple that I returned forthwith. Also if you see anything advertised that you would like to read and review, just tell her and she will order off after it. She is very nice about that and has gotten several for me. I reviewed the Baron's letters and sent it to her some time ago but they haven't used it—I quoted that nice advice of his about never opening a Catholic paper or joining a Eucharistic guild. I await its appearance with interest.*

*See review of June 23, 1956.

Letters from Baron Friedrich von Hügel to a Niece

Edited with an introduction by Gwendolen Greene. Regnery, 1955.

The Bulletin, June 23, 1956

A protestant minister once remarked to the reviewer that he had never met an American Catholic priest who had read Baron von Hügel. Since Friedrich von Hügel is frequently considered, along with Newman and Acton, as one of the great Catholic scholars, it is to be hoped that the minister's acquaintance with priests was limited. With the publication of Baron von Hügel's letters to his niece, this great man and his vigorous, intelligent piety may become better known to Americans.

The letters were written to Gwendolen Greene, then about thirty and an Anglican. Baron von Hügel's intention was to strengthen her religious sense by guiding her reading, largely in non-religious subjects. He warns her against the mentality that reads only religious literature, however good, and allows the fascinations of Grace to deaden the expressions of nature and thereby "lose the material for Grace to work on." Warning her against this, he says, "how thin and abstract, or how strained and unattractive, the religion of most women becomes, owing to this their elimination of religion's materials and divinely intended tensions!"

He advises her also not to be "churchy," to love Holy Communion but "tactfully, unironically, to escape from all Eucharistic Guilds . . . to care for God's work in the world . . . and yet (again quite silently, with full contrary encouragement to others who are helped by such literature) never opening a Church paper or magazine." This last piece of advice, so gallantly subversive to the organizational appetite, may explain handily why Baron von Hügel has not been widely read in American Catholic circles, but the reader who has been fed (sufficiently) on Irish piety may find Baron von Hügel's letters a welcome relief.

His niece became a Roman Catholic two years after his death.

Letter to "A," July 13, 1956

I read the review in The Bulletin *with much hoorawing and good cheer. . . . BUT to what horror was my pleasure turned when I then came upon Wenonah, with her blood-curdling poise, writing about Family Limitation. This, says I, is too much. My grip on reality is loosening. Who is she? Who am I? Then after hours of painful thought, it came to me that the solution must be two Wenonahs; i.e., she must have a mother. They write just alike but one must be Wenonah Sr. and the other Little Wenonah. I intend to interrogate Mrs. Hall on this subject just as soon as I can think of a tactful way to do it. I don't want the good lady to think I am criticizing her book section but then, if this is Wenonah Age 13, writing about Family Limitation, I am going to have to revise all my concepts about Catholic education, and it is going to be some time before I regain my balance.*

Beyond the Dreams of Avarice

Russell Kirk. Regnery, 1956.

The Bulletin, July 21, 1956

Monsignor Guardini has written that "when a man accepts divine truth in the obedience of faith, he is forced to rethink human truth," and it is such a rethinking in the obedience to divine truth which must be the mainspring of any enlightened social thought, whether it tends to be liberal or conservative. Since the Enlightenment, liberalism in its extreme forms has not accepted divine truth and the conservatism which has enjoyed any popularity has shown no tendency to rethink human truth or to reexamine human society. Mr. Kirk has managed in a succession of books which have proved both scholarly and popular to do both and to make the voice of an intelligent and vigorous conservative thought respected in this country.

"Beyond the Dreams of Avarice" is a collection of his essays which have appeared during the last ten years in England and America. The title is a phrase of Dr. Johnson's and it is high praise to say of Mr. Kirk's books that Dr. Johnson would almost certainly admire them, both for their thought and the vigor with which it is expressed; and Mr. Kirk confesses himself happily to be "one of those scholars whom John Dewey detested"—high praise also, although in this case Mr. Kirk is bestowing it on himself.

The essays range from a consideration of Orestes Brownson's ideas of a just society to a handy return of Dr. Kinsey to the field of zoology; but in spite of the merits of the contents, a better introduction to Mr. Kirk as a writer would be any of his other books—"The Conservative Mind," "A Program for Conservatives," or "Academic Freedom"—since a collection of reviews and magazine articles is necessarily repetitious and occasional.

In Soft Garments

Second Edition.
Ronald Knox. Sheed & Ward, 1956.

The Bulletin, August 4, 1956

This is a collection of conferences given by Monsignor Knox during the years 1926–38 to undergraduates when he was chaplain at Oxford. When the Holy See gave permission for Catholics to matriculate at Oxford and Cambridge, the stipulation was made that lectures be provided for them "to safeguard their faith in an uncongenial atmosphere." Something of the kind is needed by American Catholic students attending secular education institutions and while these lectures were specifically designed for British students more than twenty years ago, they deal with the essentials of the Faith and will have value for any Catholic reader at any time. Since the American Catholic student has always been able to attend non-Catholic universities, the uncongeniality of the atmosphere in such places may be less than apparent to him and proportionately more dangerous. The Newman Club, being generally geared more to social than intellectual considerations, does not serve the purpose as well as such lectures as these.

As Monsignor Knox puts it: "It is the nature of the undergraduate to discuss all things in heaven and earth with the utmost seriousness and sometimes with very slight information." The problem of the student attending a secular university after a predominantly Catholic education is different from that of the student who has gone to public schools all his life. The former is apt to be long on information and argument but short on perception and tact; the latter will have learned how not to offend the non-Christian sensibility but may not be well enough informed on the particulars of his Faith to maintain his own position with the necessary vigor. Monsignor Knox's conferences will provide help for both, for he deals with apologetics with perception and urbanity and with a laudable absence of unction.

The Catholic Companion to the Bible

Ralph L. Woods. Lippincott, 1956.

The Bulletin, September 1, 1956

In the introduction to this anthology, Bishop John Wright suggests that the reason Catholics are "frequently less articulate about their love for the Bible than other Christian peoples . . . may be the presence among Catholics of an awe, reverential and profound, which makes them feel humble in the presence of this mighty compendium of divine revelation and sacred mysteries." This statement would seem to be the extreme example of looking at our sins through stained glass windows. Catholics who are not articulate about their love of the Bible are generally those who do not love it, since they read it as seldom as possible, and those who don't read the Bible do not read it because of laziness or indifference or the fear that reading it will endanger their faith, not the Catholic faith but faith itself. It is the latter difficulty which this book would help to alleviate.

In the scientistic atmosphere of this century, the Bible can be a stumbling block to the faith of those who are not equipped with an adequate knowledge of the nature of inspiration and prophecy, the dates of the books and gospels, and the literary modes of the authors, their use of allegory, metaphor, and history.

The present volume contains articles and quotations by Catholic writers from St. Jerome to Dom Van Zeller. These seem generally too short to give the reader more than an interest in finding a longer and more comprehensive treatment elsewhere, but the book has the value of any anthology, along with its grab-bag character. It will be a stimulant, a good beginning, a companion as the title suggests; but Catholic residents of the Bible Belt will find it expedient to go further.

Letter to "A," September 8, 1956

So [Mrs. Hall] wants 200 words only? Well, the difference between 200 words and one page (the original stipulation) is 50 words so all you have to do is leave out the conjunctions. She has not told me this new ruling yet; in fact, she has ignored me entirely lately and I haven't got a book in two months anyway. I am afraid I cooked my goose with her by asking for The Metamorphic Tradition in Modern Poetry.* *She's never printed the review. Anyway, I sympathize with her about the 200 words. 200 words is enough. These aren't reviews, just notices, and what you need to develop for them is something I call Church Prose (from Church Mouse)—lean spare poor and hungry. It's no great question of art here though you can say one or two pertinent things with 200 words. Me, I have a hard time making some of my reviews even that long. But this is something that has apparently plagued her all along as she told me when she first started writing me that most of the reviews were too long. I guess she was giving me fair warning.*

*See review of January 5, 1957.

The Archbishop and the Lady

Michael de la Bedoyere. Pantheon, 1956.

The Bulletin, September 29, 1956

This is an account of the persecution of Madame Guyon, the author of the "Moyen Court," and Fenelon, Archbishop of Cambrai, by the French court and clergy in the 17th century. In these times when every newspaper advertises that Christ is the way to success, it is particularly cheering to have this story reconstructed, for as the parties to the conflict were drawn more and more closely to the Divine, they enjoyed less and less success in the world, Fenelon being deprived of just ambitions both for himself and the future of France and Madame Guyon eventually spending eight years in the Bastille.

Besides recounting this engrossing story, the author throws considerable light on the subject of true and false mysticism and shows clearly that Madame Guyon, although an emotional and bizarre woman given to an inflated style of writing, never deviated in intention from the mainstream of mystical doctrine taught by the Church. Essentially she practiced the "little way" that St. Thérèse of Lisieux, with possibly an even ghastlier style of writing, was to make more widely known to the world two centuries later. Madame Guyon, however, had an unfortunate period of history in which to publish her way of prayer, and for an enemy one of the most famous Catholic bishops of all time, Bossuet, who emerges from this study something less than respectable.

The author points out that "there can, of course, be no certainty in the reconstruction of disputed points in the small amount of historical testimony which posterity possesses," but throughout his conclusions seem fair and indisputable.

Meditations Before Mass

Romano Guardini. Newman, 1955.

The Bulletin, November 24, 1956

The title in this case does not mean meditations to be made by the faithful before the celebration of the Mass but meditations on the nature of the Mass in an attempt to restore it to its proper perspective for the individual and the congregation and the Church making its way in history. This is a task that must be reaccomplished continually and always in the relation of the Mass to Truth which, Monsignor Guardini points out, "piety is inclined to neglect. . . . Not that it shuns or shies away from it, but it is remarkable how readily piety slides off into fantasy, sentimentality and exaggeration. Legends and devotional books offer only too frequent and devastating proof of this; unfortunately piety is inclined to lose itself in the subjective, to become musty, turgid, unspiritual. Divine reality is never any of these. . . ."

One of the most useful chapters, in so far as being a corrective to a popular abuse of the Mass, is the one concerned with the hindrance of sentimentality, which Monsignor Guardini defines as "the desire to be moved." Other chapters, particularly in the second half of the book, are more profound. The first half is concerned with the attitude necessary for a full participation; the second considers "the Lord's memorial itself, not for the sake of theoretical information, but in order to prepare us for the holy act." At one point Monsignor Guardini says that the words spoken at the consecration are "the equals of those which once brought the universe into existence." Whatever his subject, he constantly illuminates it with such insights.

Monsignor Guardini is Professor of Philosophy at the University of Munich and was named House Chaplain to the Pope in 1952.

reviews and letters

1957

The Metamorphic Tradition in Modern Poetry

Sister Bernetta Quinn. Rutgers, 1955.

The Bulletin, January 5, 1957

According to the introduction, "the principal aim of 'The Metamorphic Tradition in Modern Poetry' is to give a sense of direction in the exploration of what to many readers is a New World, the world of contemporary verse." Such a statement might suggest that Sister Bernetta's essays are for the uninformed or for those who are only now being introduced to modern poetry; however, only the well-informed reader already acquainted with the longer works of Pound, Stevens, Eliot, Yeats, Crane, Jarrell and Williams will be interested in these essays, behind or in which lurks the not very well laid ghost of a doctoral dissertation. The newcomer to modern verse will be frightened away.

Sister Bernetta considers these seven poets according to a variety of metamorphic elements which appear in their work and she does it with scholarship and thoroughness and with a sympathy for the poetry for which we may be grateful. The essays seem to be valuable ground work but to lack what would stimulate an interest in these poets if one is not already present. Remarking that the book does not have a definite enough underlying structure, R. W. B. Lewis, writing in the *Kenyon Review*, says that the "difficulty is not at all any 'Catholic bias'; oddly enough it is rather the contrary.

Sister Bernetta does not by any means impose a Catholic structure on her materials. In my opinion, she muzzles her Thomism overmuch." This is interesting, particularly to the reader who has often seen a "Catholic structure" used like a bulldozer to undermine the work. It may be an awareness of this danger that has made Sister Bernetta overcareful in avoiding tools that she might otherwise have made good use of. In any case, we may be grateful to find a Sister of Saint Francis writing with sympathy about the poetry of Ezra Pound and Hart Crane and hope that this foreshadows some happy metamorphosis in the general state of literary appreciation by Catholics.

A Path through Genesis

Bruce Vawter, C.M. Sheed & Ward, 1956.

The Bulletin, January 19, 1957

In the epilogue to this book, Father Vawter writes "The end of the Bible must be our beginning. This is why there must be no shrinking from a truly scientific study of the Bible." The present volume is Father Vawter's summarization of the scientific study by the Church's scholars on the book of Genesis, and should help fill the Catholic's great need for a knowledge of how to interpret the Bible in the light of present day discoveries. Father Vawter's interest is to explain such distinctions as that between revelation and inspiration; to show the Biblical author's parallel use of sources and his unconcern with chronological accuracy. There is no straining here to make Genesis fit scientific facts. The effort is rather to explain how the facts the writer had at his disposal were used for an inspired religious purpose. Father Vawter points out that any interpretation that contradicts a known fact of science is no true interpretation and that we must understand the use of folk history and of the various literary forms employed by the Biblical authors before we are able to begin to comprehend what the inspired writer intended to teach. In his introduction Father Vawter notes the marked reluctance of Catholics to read the Bible in spite of encouragement and promptings by modern popes and bishops. This excellent and thoroughly readable study is probably the best kind of corrective for that tendency.

The Two-Edged Sword

John L. McKenzie, S.J. Bruce, 1956.

The Bulletin, January 19, 1957

This is a spiritual interpretation of the Old Testament from the standpoint of the most recent biblical scholarship. To understand the uniqueness of God's revelation to the Hebrews, it is necessary to have some knowledge of the ancient cults that surround them. This is also perhaps the best way to avoid fundamentalist interpretations and literal readings which confuse fiction with fact and figure with reality. Our age is more aware of the human element in the composition of the Bible than past ages have been. As the author points out, " . . . our own generation must read the Bible in its own way. Our difficulties in understanding the Bible must arise from our times, our education, our culture, and we must meet these difficulties ourselves."

Because the Old Testament raises doubts in the minds of many, many do not read it; few Catholics, in fact, receive any training in how it should be read. The author declares that the biblical scholar cannot, nor should be expected to, resolve every line-by-line difficulty, for the Bible should be read first in the security of the faith which the Church has given. Granted this, the biblical scholar is in a better position than the spiritual writer to aid the faithful in returning to frequent Bible reading, and the great value of this particular book, besides scholarship and style, is that it will produce in the reader a desire to go at once to the Old Testament and make himself acquainted with it first hand.

Writings of Edith Stein

Edited and Translated by Hilda Graef. Newman, 1956.

The Bulletin, March 2, 1957

This is a selection of the writings of Edith Stein, a German Jewish philosopher who became a Catholic in 1922, subsequently entered the Carmelite Order and died in the gas chambers at Auschwitz in 1942. The selections have been made, translated and introduced by Hilda Graef whose biography of the author, "The Scholar and the Cross," appeared a year or two ago. The selections have apparently been made in order to show the range of Edith Stein's personality and scholarship; a sampling is given from her spiritual, mystical, educational, and philosophical writings, but in each case not a large enough sample to do more than tantalize the reader who has a real interest in the subject she is writing about.

The spiritual writings, of which only three examples are given, are very impressive, being the type of spirituality that is based on thought rather than emotion. The mystical writings include an essay on the Pseudo-Dionysius which is perhaps the most interesting piece in the book. The educational writings reveal the author to have been a thoroughgoing feminist, willing when the occasion demanded to wrestle with the Apostle Paul. The philosophical writings will probably be of interest only to those who have a background in the phenomenological approach of Edmund Husserl whose student and assistant Edith Stein was in her early days.

This is a valuable book in as much as it is at present all that is available to us of Edith Stein's work in translation.

The Spirit and Forms of Protestantism

Rev. Louis Bouyer. Newman, 1956.

The Bulletin, April 27, 1957

Father Bouyer, a priest of the French Oratory, was brought up a Protestant and was for some years a Lutheran minister. In seeking the heart of Protestantism, he was led to the Church and found in Catholicism the only Church where the positive principles of the Reformation could find fulfillment. He makes it plain that he has never rejected his Protestant upbringing or those positive principles of Luther and Calvin or the later Protestant revival of John Wesley.

He begins by affirming that the Reformation must be understood in the light of certain positive assertions of Christianity which the Catholic Church has never denied. His explanation of why a reform which set out from such principles could end in schism and heresy is that embedded in the positive principles were certain negative ones that came from the decadent scholasticism of the 15th century. The apologists of the Counter-Reformation era, being themselves imprisoned in this nominalist philosophy, were unable to offer effective criticism. The real issues could not be seen by either side.

This is a book which should be important in the education of every Catholic. Too often books issuing from Catholic sources on the subject of Protestantism are narrow, overbearing and totally ineffective by virtue of the type of polemic which aims to crush rather than understand the opposition. Father Bouyer's book has the merit of his experience and he sees as opposed to the Church only those elements in Protestantism which oppose it to itself.

Criticism and Censorship

Walter F. Kerr. Bruce, 1956.

The Bulletin, May 11, 1957

The present volume makes up the fifth Gabriel Richard Lecture and was delivered by Mr. Kerr, the drama critic for the New York *Herald Tribune*, at Trinity College in 1954. Along with the recent address of Fr. John Courtney Murray on the subject of censorship in a pluralistic society, this lecture probably exhibits the most intelligent approach to censorship that one is presently liable to get from Catholic writers on the subject. While admitting the necessity of censorship, Mr. Kerr deplores its practice by unauthorized groups in what is called pre-censorship, a custom which has created the tendency to make every man a censor with a "watchdog" attitude toward art. Mr. Kerr says "the generally low taste of the Catholic community in America has been a minor scandal for quite some time now. It stares at us from the pages of the same diocesan newspapers that devote so much of their space to censorial exhortation." That is a sentence that would deserve prompt publication even if the rest of the lecture did not. Mr. Kerr goes on to say that "to inhibit taste one must first kill love; after that, distinctions won't matter. I suspect then that the generally low level of Catholic taste is not something that has simply happened . . . ; it is more likely something that has been created, a kind of paralysis born of inculcated fear." Along with the low level of taste, Mr. Kerr says, goes the confidence that it need not be improved. "Fear has cut off that natural affection which might have produced natural taste; indifference has cut off that serious study which might have produced knowledge. The subject of art, in all of its aspects, is conveniently kept at arm's length."

This book can be recommended as a study manual for all NCCW decent literature committees.

A Popular History of the Reformation

Philip Hughes. Hanover, 1957.

The Bulletin, June 8, 1957

"Popular" in this case must mean abbreviated, though it may also be assumed that a history has to be abbreviated in order to be popular; but Father Hughes is such an excellent historian that it is difficult to see how any reader could prefer these abridgments (Father Hughes also has a "Popular History of the Catholic Church") to the author's longer studies.

The present volume deals with the state of Catholic life in Europe before the Reformation, with Luther and the first Protestants, with the English Reformation, Calvin, the Council of Trent, and finally with Knox. The first sections appear almost leisurely and are most satisfying; the second half of the book is so obviously an abridgment that the reader may occasionally wonder where he is at. By the time he reaches John Knox, the pace is so terrific that that figure is barely glimpsed in dashing by.

The monumental* task of condensing these histories into single volumes could perhaps not have been accomplished at all by a scholar and writer of less than Father Hughes' stature, but it might be questioned if this kind of labor is worth his time. A great merit of the book will at least be to lure the reader to seek out his longer works.

*Published "momentual."

God the Unknown

Victor White, O.P. Harper, 1956.

The Inner Search

Hubert Van Zeller, O.S.B. Sheed & Ward, 1957.

Occult Phenomena

Dr. Alois Wiesinger, O.C.S.O. Newman, 1957.

The Bulletin, June 8, 1957

Although these three books were read together by chance, they invite review together because all three throw light from different angles on the subject of the unknown God. Father White explores the subject from the objective theological side. Father Van Zeller from the side of man's individual search, and Father Wiesinger obliquely by a consideration of those occult phenomena which give hints of the powers of man before the Fall.

Father White's book is a collection of essays delivered at various places rather than an extended consideration of the unknown God. In his introduction, the author recognized that the essay is an inadequate medium for exhaustive treatment of profound theological subjects but that it may meet the needs of the inquirer who is unable to give them sustained attention. It is good to have these pieces collected, for Father White is an excellent scholar and writer, but the title of the book is misleading and individual essays will prove more valuable than the book as a whole.

Van Zeller writes about the individual soul searching for the hidden God in the circumstances of life and through the Church in prayer and the sacraments. This is one of those books which, lacking a definite intellectual problem to attack, is, in spite of its wisdom, apt to prove dull if read longer than ten minutes at a time. The ideal form for unadulterated wisdom is the aphorism.

Dr. Wiesinger is a theologian who is versed in the findings of depth psychology and parapsychology, and in "Occult Phenomena" he deals with the subject of mysterious manifestations ranging from telepathy and clairvoyance to the secondary phenomena in genuine mystical experience. He believes that all such manifestations are examples of gifts which were possessed by man before the Fall and which now appear as rudiments of those powers. These can act only when the spiritual part of the soul is partly released from the body as in sleep, trance, hypnosis, etc. This theory removes us from the extremes of spiritualism and demonomania and is in line with the Church's teaching to regard all such phenomena as natural until it is proven otherwise. The book is particularly interesting in the distinctions it makes between trance and the last stages of mystical experience. It leaves the reader with a sense of the unknown God by providing him with a sense of the largely unexplored activities of the spirit-soul.

The Holy Fire

Robert Payne. Harper, 1957.

The Bulletin, July 20, 1957

This is a book containing short biographies of ten Fathers of the Eastern Church, beginning with Clement of Alexandria in the second century and closing with Gregory Palamas in the fourteenth. As the author points out, the Fathers of the Eastern Church sometimes seem remote from us. "Their Christianity is not the same as ours. They were a people of warm imaginations, more incandescent than the Fathers of the Western Church, fiercer in denunciation, quicker in anger, more sudden to praise. They stressed many things we have left unstressed." However this may be, these early Fathers probably contributed as much to the development of Christian thought as Augustine and Jerome, and certainly Dionysius the Areopagite, as the author himself declares, influenced mystical theology in the West as much as any Western Father. Altogether, the separation the author makes between their Christianity and ours would seem to be exaggerated.

The Catholic reader will also mark the author's loose use of such words as "worship." In several instances he gives the impression that relics were worshiped in the early Church, rather than venerated. Excessive devotion may have been tolerated locally at various times, but he does not make it clear that image and relic worship are not parts of Christian doctrine.

The best parts of the book are contributed by the Eastern Fathers when Mr. Payne allows them to speak for themselves. Fortunately, he is liberal in his use of quotations.

God's Heralds

J. C. Chaine. Translated by Brendan McGrath, O.S.B. Wagner, 1955.

The Bulletin, August 3, 1957

The purpose of this book is to assist those who wish to read the prophetic literature of the Old Testament by furnishing them with the relevant historical, cultural and religious background material. Read in conjunction with the Prophets, such a book can be an invaluable aid in deepening appreciation of prophetic revelation and the conditions under which this was given to the world. As the translator points out in the preface, "The world of the prophets is a complicated one, and it takes serious study to become really familiar with it."

The author was for many years until his death in 1948 Professor of Scripture at Lyon, first at the Grand Seminary and then in the Faculte's catholiques [*sic*]. The present work has no counterpart in English by a Catholic.

Essays and Addresses on the Philosophy of Religion

Volumes 1 and 2
Friedrich von Hügel. Dutton, 1950.

The Bulletin, August 31, 1957

The writings of Baron von Hügel have apparently been little read in this country by Catholics in spite of the reissue in 1955 of his "Letters to a Niece" by Regnery and the Thomas

More Association. This is unfortunate because a consideration of the always measured and intellectually just tone of his essays on religious subjects would serve as an antidote to the frequently superficial methods by which many popular American Catholic writers approach and sidestep the problems of faith or meet them with the Instant Answer.

In his introduction, von Hügel says that there is not a "paper here which does not raise more questions than it solves . . . "—a characteristic which the reader will observe to be the opposite of that found in much of our current writing on religion, where the solution is put forth without giving the reader any sense that the question has been experienced.

Reading the works of Baron von Hügel, the reader always has the sense that the question has been experienced and that it has made its mark on the man. This quality is perhaps in part accounted for by Baron von Hügel's active sense of the historic. He trusts that there is "not a line printed within these covers but is steeped in this sense of Conditions, Growth, Contingencies," but it is in greater part accounted for by a genuine encounter with the Church, a wrestling with it, a love tested by considerable adversity. For those wishing to learn of these aspects of his life, the definitive biography by Michael da la Bedoyere is available from Scribners.

The essays in these two volumes concern themselves with such subjects as religion and illusion, religion and reality. Of the two series, the first is the more interesting and would be of more profit to the general reader. Although von Hügel's Germanic style is often cumbersome, his essays are immanently [*sic*] readable.

The Ordeal of Gilbert Pinfold

Evelyn Waugh. Little, Brown, 1957.

Give Me Possession

Paul Horgan. Farrar, Straus & Cudahy, 1957.

The Bulletin, October 12, 1957

"The Ordeal of Gilbert Pinfold," a conversation piece as the author calls it, recounts the hallucinations of a middle-aged author aboard a ship bound for Ceylon, an experience similar to which Mr. Waugh himself claims to have undergone several years ago. He feels that others who have had hallucinations of this kind will find the novel amusing. Whether this is a necessary requirement for finding it amusing he does not say. The book is worked out with the usual finesse that one might expect from a writer of his quality and it is always good to see even a slight book as this done with style and a certain flourish. However, even for those of us who have hallucinations regularly, the conversation piece may seem to go on for a chapter or two longer than necessary. Mr. Waugh writes some very funny sentences, such as, "A funereal limousine bore them to Kew," which may be taken out of context and enjoyed without regard to the rest of the book.

Mr. Horgan's novel, on the other hand, is serious in intent. It details the gradual realization by a wealthy and rather silly couple that their barely conscious materialism is not sufficient to live by, that they must take possibility instead of possession, or, as advised by a priest who figures in the action "find a new faith." This theme becomes fairly obtrusive in the last part of the book, where the bones of symbol and allegory begin to stick out alarmingly. The first part, however, and particularly a section that concerns existence at a fashionable boys' school in the west, is in the best satirical tradition and a great pleasure to read. This section, more than the book as a whole, makes the theme convincing and never states it.

Letters to Men and Women

François de Salignac de La Mothe Fénelon. Newman, 1957.

The Character of Man

Emmanuel Mounier. Harper, 1957.

Lines of Life

François Mauriac. Farrar, Straus & Cudahy, 1957.

The Bulletin, October 26, 1957

Although one of these books is a collection of letters written in the 17th century, one a scientific work, and one a novel, they are all three remarkably alike in spirit and all three have as an underlying concern the entrance of love into the world through the medium of the human character despite its natural distortions.

Fénelon's letters are directed to lay men and women who wish to achieve holiness in the world and who must combat, in addition to their internal distortions of character, the distortions of 17th century French court society. The letters show a marked respect for the individual temperament and a delicacy of approach that gives them a lasting value, both as literature and as spiritual direction. It is interesting to note that Emmanuel Mounier, in his scientific study of man's character, has occasion at least once to quote from Fénelon's letters. Mounier's personalist approach is closely akin to Fénelon's courtesy.

Mounier's study, reduced here from its 800 original pages to 314, is a compendium of the contributions of modern psychology to the study of the person, from the purely physical aspects of man, to his spiritual possibilities within the limits of character. The first chapter, titled, "Toward the Mystery of the Person," is perhaps an adequate description of the direction of the entire book and confirms the author's contention that his science, though honest, "is a fighting science." He is fighting for the mystery of the person as against any kind of determination, though always within the limits of the given. There is little doubt that this book is, as claimed on the jacket, the major work of "one of the really great men of our time." The only pity about this edition is that it has been so drastically abridged.

The distortions that François Mauriac has frequently concerned himself with in his fictions are the distortions in the lives of what Mounier would call "the moral gentry." In this novel he is occupied with the difficulty of the acceptance, even the recognition, of Grace by those whose lives have been deadened with the kind of morality and pious habit which has no basis in genuine charity. "Lines of Life" was first published in the early twenties under the title "Destins" and has since been twice translated into English. It tells of a middle-aged woman whose life is momentarily disrupted by her peculiar attraction for a degenerate boy, an attraction which breaks up for a short space of time the patterns of religious complacency in which she has been immured. By the end of the novel, however, she has almost forgotten her peculiar experience and is again "one of those dead carried down the stream of life."

These are three extremely valuable books.

St. John of the Cross

Bruno de Jesus Marie, O.C.D. Sheed & Ward, 1957.

Doctor Rabelais

D. B. Wyndham Lewis. Sheed & Ward, 1957.

The Bulletin, December 21, 1957

This definitive life of St. John of the Cross has a valuable introduction by Jacques Maritain and a postscript by the editor, Father Benedict Zimmerman. The postscript could well be read before the main body of the work as it summarizes in a clear fashion the history of the Reform of the Carmelite Order in Spain in the 16th century. This is a tortuous history and without a summary of it, the reader will frequently be lost in this particular biography. The author made use of the latest discovered documents at the time of writing—the translation was made in 1932—and for those interested in research on the subject, the work will be valuable and necessary. The scholarship is thorough but the presentation is often fuzzy. Most of the notes are in Spanish. There is a good deal of place description which is tedious and no monk or nun but who passed in front of the saint fails to be named and described. St. John of the Cross does emerge from all this but not so solidly as in some of Father Bruno's shorter essays on various aspects of his subject.

It is a good deal easier to write a biography of a scoundrel than a saint, even when not as much is known about him. What is known of Rabelais would fill a few pages but Mr. D. B. Wyndham Lewis has pursued his subject through 250. Rabelais began his clerical life as a Franciscan, switched to the Benedictines, switched to the regular clergy, and it is not known finally whether he died in or out of the Church, but Mr. Lewis's effort has largely been to show that his subject was no hero of enlightenment in the 16th century but a rather ordinary opportunist with a great comic genius. In this he succeeds to the reader's satisfaction and since he has a high appreciation of Rabelais' gift, his argument fortunately escapes the sound of special pleading.

How to Read a Novel

Caroline Gordon. Viking, 1957.

Unpublished Review

By now all are familiar with the famous ad found in a diocesan paper: "Let a Catholic do your termite work." In connection with literature, which is almost as dangerous as termites, this fraternal attitude abounds. Miss Gordon's book can therefore be recommended on the grounds that it is a Catholic who is writing. It would be painful to leave it at this.

As Miss Gordon points out, it requires a certain humility to read a novel; and perhaps also it requires a certain humility to read a book called *How to Read a Novel,* for everyone thinks novel-reading well within his competence. This book should satisfy any reader that it is not; and it can be particularly recommended for Catholics because Catholic groups are often vocal on the subject of "bad" literature, without knowing "good" literature when they see it. To pronounce judgment on a novel, one must first be able to read it. The suspicion with which the average Catholic approaches this particular art form is lessened only if the label Catholic can be applied to it in some way. Those moral principles which save us from counting ourselves among the admirers of such works as *Peyton Place* seldom operate in more subtle cases of corruption. We are liable to praise prose as poor, structure as weak, and psychology as dishonest if only the characters involved live, or at least die, according to the precepts of the Church. This is a cultural deficiency but it implies and it fosters a lack of moral insight.

No one will go through Miss Gordon's book and begin forthwith to read adequately, but he will begin to read more slowly and some of the fiction which satisfied him before will no longer do so. This book, along with Maritain's *Art and Scholasticism*, should be studied by any Catholic group making public pronouncements about literature.

reviews and letters

1958

The Roots of the Reformation Karl Adam.
Marriage and the Family Francis J. Sheed.
Confession John C. Heenan.
The Rosary Maisie Ward.
The Devil Walter Farrell.
Canterbury Books, Sheed & Ward.

The Bulletin, January 4, 1958

These five titles are the first issues in a new series called Canterbury Books published by Sheed & Ward. The "series is designed for those who want a more complete treatment of a subject than is possible in a pamphlet but who do not want to search for it among much else . . . in a full-length book." Since these were all excellent books to begin with, the selections from them are naturally valuable, but the question which comes to the reviewer's mind is whether the editors think the Catholic reader is too idiotic to read an index and find what interests him in a complete book; or if he is such a person of affairs that he has time only for selected aspects of a subject. A second question is whether these books could not have been published as full-length paper-back books at very little more expense to publisher and reader. Karl Adam's *The Spirit of Catholicism* was published as a full-length paper-back and sold for 75¢. In this series we have four chapters from Adam's *One and Holy* for 75¢.

It is possible that books on the rosary and confession, appealing only to a Catholic audience, might have such a small sale that this type of publishing would be necessary; but for books of interest to a wider audience—books on the Reformation, marriage, and the devil—one wonders if larger sales would not make it possible for the complete books to be offered at the same or slightly higher price.

Mr. John Delaney of Doubleday & Company said on a recent Catholic Hour broadcast that the "heavier" Image Books, such as the *Summa Contra Gentiles* have been equal in sales and demand with the "lighter" types such as *Father Malachy's Miracle.* "Surprisingly," he said, "St. Thomas has outsold Bruce Marshall." This is cheering news and indicates that Catholic books can find a market with the non-Catholic reader when they are good books. It also indicates that the Catholic reader may be interested in complete books rather than these truncated editions.

Prayer in Practice

Romano Guardini. Pantheon, 1957.

The Bulletin, February 22, 1958

Although he speaks in general terms, Monsignor Guardini makes the major emphasis of this book on prayer its purpose and practice by the individual. He is a writer acutely sensitive to the personal in religious problems and he points out that the only purpose of discipline in prayer is to safeguard its freedom. "The sincerer it is, the less can we prescribe how it should be done; it assumes the form appropriate to the individual's inner condition, to his experience, and the circumstances in which he stands." This being the case, he makes it clear that many of the prayers found in current prayer books are not only useless to the development of the life of prayer but positively harmful. "Many of these prayers are simply superfluous; others affect our spirit as bad food affects our body. Prayer . . . must above all be truthful." He speaks of having a "sense of honor" in prayer, a sense which will be offended by the mawkish, sentimental and exaggerated. He also reminds the reader that "In the writings of the saints we frequently come across strong passages expressing self-contempt and self-abasement. These . . . must be understood . . . as expressions of the personality of the saint. They cannot be held as applying to all conditions of life, nor must they be interpreted as forming part of the basic attitude and mood of Christian life."

From a discussion of oral prayer, he goes on to consider contemplative prayer and the relation of faith to prayer. He discusses the problem of those whose faith is so insufficient that they cannot pray with sincerity. His concerns are very much for the problems of modern man, in whom faith is often no more than a possibility. It is, in part, the realization of the modern condition that makes all of Monsignor Guardini's work so vital.

Come South Wind

Edited by M. L. Shrady. Pantheon, 1957.

The Bulletin, February 22, 1958

This is a collection of writings by various contemplatives ranging from St. Augustine to Martin D'Arcy, S.J., who also contributes an introduction. In this he remarks about the sense of family likeness that he felt between the selections in the book. The reader too may be struck by this but may wonder if it is altogether a virtue. Thomas Merton is represented five times while St. Teresa of Avila is not included,

Ruysbroeck, Tauler, and Eckhart are well represented but St. Thomas Aquinas has not managed to get in. The emphasis would seem to be on the mystic whose expression tends to poetry. Since the anthology does not claim to be comprehensive and the selections are dependent on the taste of the editor, no justified complaint can be made; nevertheless, one wonders about any anthology of contemplative writings in which there are no selections from St. Catherine of Siena, St. Catherine of Genoa, or St. Teresa of Avila.

The Meeting of Love and Knowledge

M. C. D'Arcy, S.J. Harper, 1957.

The Christ of Faith

Karl Adam. Pantheon, 1957.

The Bulletin, April 5, 1958

Following Arnold Toynbee, Aldous Huxley and others, there is much current interest in a syncretist religion which would incorporate what Huxley calls "the perennial wisdom"—the highest common ideals in Hinduism, Buddhism and Christianity. Father D'Arcy's reasoned argument is that, though there is much to be gained from the East, there is no highest common denominator among these religions. With the Eastern religions it is a matter of extinguishing individuality and desire; with the Christian of fulfilling them. "Without persons and personality there is no Christian religion, and its philosophy centers around this thought that, whereas in brute matter anonymity reigns rather than individuality, as we ascend the scale, separate individualities emerge until in man selfhood is found, the image of that life where the richest personality abounds." In Buddhism this world and the self are finally of no account.

The best way to understand the uniqueness of Christianity is by a proper Christology. Although not concerned with syncretist thought, Karl Adam's *The Christ of Faith* provides the best argumentation of the impossibility of Christianity's being fused into a syncretist religion. This book is a Christology of the living Church, based on tradition and dogma rather than on a reconstruction of Christ's times as in Daniel-Rops' *Jesus and His Times* or on spiritual intuition as in Monsignor Guardini's *The Lord*. Its base of operation is the fact that the Church knows Christ "out of her living self-awareness which through the centuries is its own ever renewed testimony." It is particularly valuable in its criticism of the errors of liberal theology, pointing out that the textual critic assumes that Christianity is something finished and inflexible and has poured all its vitality into its literature and foundations and become fossilized in them. *The Christ of Faith* is a master work by one of the Church's greatest living theologians.

The Transgressor

Julian Green. Pantheon, 1957.

The Bulletin, May 3, 1958

Spokesmen for the deliver-us-from-gloom school of Catholic criticism have found that this novel commits the unpardonable sin: it is depressing. It presents the situation of a young girl, innocent and lacking all spiritual resources, who conceives a passion for a man who not only cannot love her but who is, in addition, thoroughly evil. It proceeds to detail her gradual realization of evil until the point when, penetrated by what remains a purely mental knowledge of it, she kills herself. She is surrounded throughout by a cast of characters of whom the best lack power to help her and the worst contrive to force her situation.

Some slight criticism can be made of the book on literary grounds. The reader is asked to believe in a passion which, while possible, is not adequately dramatized in its beginnings. We are told, not shown, that in a matter of minutes such a love is conceived by the girl. In the rest of the novel we are most adequately shown the results of it but the book would have proceeded on a less shaky foundation had the scene in which the girl's infatuation began been presented. However, Mr. Green is such an excellent writer that he manages to overcome most of the problems presented by his situation. The novel is written with great deftness and delicacy and with a moral awareness that comes only with long contemplation on the nature of charity. It presents the kind of situation which emphasizes the mystery of evil in its starkest aspects and it offers no solutions by the author in the name of God; nor does it offer the solutions of faith for those who do not believe. It is completely lacking in false piety and is in every sense a book which has derived from the best type of Catholic imagination.

Painting and Reality

Étienne Gilson. Pantheon, 1957.

The Bulletin, May 3, 1958

This is an exhaustive exposition of the kind of reality proper to paintings and of the relation of painting to the other arts and to the natural order. M. Gilson begins by describing the physical nature of paintings and goes on to the more abstract considerations only after this thorough groundwork has been constructed. His touchstones are the writings of the great painters themselves, da Vinci, Constable, Klee, but most notably Delacroix whose journals he obviously admires considerably.

The most valuable part of the book is the discussion of modern painting contained in the last two chapters. The essence of the art of painting is not imitation but the creative addition of artifacts to nature. M. Gilson believes that the evolution of modern painting has been a process of freeing it from the burden of imitation which was laid on it in the Renaissance. In his words: "Reduced to its simplest expression, the function of modern art has been to restore painting to its primitive and true function, which is to continue through man the creative activity of nature. In so doing, modern painting has destroyed nothing and condemned nothing that belongs in any one of the legitimate activities of man; it has simply regained the clear awareness of its own nature and recovered its own place among the creative activities of man."

There are 117 illustrations in half-tone plates and an appendix containing selections from the writings of Reynolds, Delacroix, Gill and Ozenfant.

Letter to "A," May 31, 1958

E. sent me the paperback Prince of Darkness *and I guess I will write a review of it. I had forgotten that only five of the stories are about the clergy and they are the only ones that are good. The other six are heaby [sic]. They just don't rise. A magazine called* Critique *put out at the University of Minnesota is going to devote its Fall 58 issue to critical articles on me and Powers. Articles by Caroline, John P. Sisk, Sr. Bernetta Quinn, Louis D. Rubin and others. It should at least be interesting to see what turns up.*

Patterns in Comparative Religion

Mircea Eliade. Sheed & Ward, 1958.

The Bulletin, July 12, 1958

This book describes various religious hierophanies—rite, myth, cosmogony, god—in relation to and as a manifestation of the mental world of those who believed in them. These hierophanies are in general alien to the Judeo-Christian religious life and, as the author points out, largely appear as aberrations to us; but one object of this study is to get away from prejudices of the lecture room and instead of considering these beliefs as pantheism, fetishism, infantilism and so on, to help the reader understand the meaning of the sacred in primitive cultures. "That the dialectic of hierophanies of the manifestation of the sacred in material things should be an object for even such complex theology as that of the Middle Ages serves to prove that it remains the cardinal problem of any religion. One might even say that all hierophanies are simply prefigurations of the miracles of the Incarnation, that every hierophany is an abortive attempt to reveal the mystery of the coming together of God and man." This is reason enough to make this kind of study valuable.

Further Paradoxes

Henri de Lubac, S.J. Newman, 1957.

The Bulletin, October 4, 1958

This is a collection of pensées and aphorisms written by Père de Lubac with the particular situation of the Church in France in mind. The author describes a paradox as "the reverse view of what, properly perceived, would be a synthesis." Synthesis is what we seek; paradox is the search for synthesis. It faces toward fulness. Paradox exists in reality before it exists in thought. Since the synthesis of the world has not been made, the universe in growth is paradoxical. "The higher life rises, the richer, the more interior it becomes, the more ground paradox gains . . . ; the mystical life is its triumph."

Fragmentary thoughts make difficult reading because the reader has to supply a context for them out of his own experience. However, this should not be hard to do even though our experience does not tally exactly with that of the Church in France. In their roots, these paradoxes are based on the experience of all thinking Christians.

American Classics Reconsidered

Edited by H. C. Gardiner, S.J. Scribners, 1958.

The Bulletin, November 1, 1958

In this collection of essays by competent Catholic literary scholars the aim, loosely, has been to reconsider 19th century American writers in the light of Catholic theology and to discover the influence of this theology on their writing. With the exception of Poe, the writers considered—Emerson, Cooper, Brownson, Hawthorne, Longfellow, Poe, Thoreau, Melville, Whitman, and the literary historians—were largely in reaction from the rapidly decaying Calvinism. They swung widely away from this to Transcendentalism, and in this process of going from one extreme to another, they touched upon or veered toward a great many pre-Reformation attitudes, residual pieties that had their roots in something deeper than Puritanism. This is not to say, as Father Gardiner, the editor, points out, that any of the writers under consideration were conscious of deeper roots or "would not have repudiated any such cultural affinity if it had been pointed out to them; it is to suggest, however, that their work can be adequately appreciated only if it is considered against an older theological and philosophical background."

Of late there has been a certain amount of renewed attention given to Christian theology and its influence on literature, and this book is a notable contribution to reestablishing a long neglected point-of-view.

Order and History

Volume 1, *Israel and Revelation*
Eric Voegelin. Louisiana State University Press, 1956.

The Bulletin, November 15, 1958

This is the first volume of a six-volume study, *Order and History*, which for both breadth of imagination and close scholarship is perhaps unequaled today by any work of comparable scope on the philosophy of history. *Israel and Revelation* begins with a consideration of the archaic cultures of the ancient Near East and their cosmological order. Voegelin considers the beginning of history as that break in civilizational development which began with Abram's exodus from Ur, continued when Israel was brought out of Egypt by Moses and became a people under God, and finally with the breakdown of the Davidic Kingdom, continued with the Prophet's movement away from the concrete Israel itself into the vision of Israel as the Suffering Servant of God. In the Hellenic world man was seeking God, in the Hebrew world God was seeking man. Real history begins when man accepts the God Who is, Who seeks him.

This monumental study, of which three volumes have so far been published, has been compared in importance to the work of Vico, Hegel, Spengler, and Toynbee. However, unlike Spengler and Toynbee, Voegelin does not see history as civilizational cycles, but as a Journey away from civilizations by a people which has taken the "leap in being," and has accepted existence under God. The study is a further advance over Toynbee in that it satisfactorily answers the comparativism which sees all spiritual movements as fundamentally the same and of equal importance. "Without Israel there would be no history, but only the eternal recurrence of societies in cosmological form."

Eric Voegelin has lately returned to the University of Munich from which he was at one time expelled by the Nazis.

Late Dawn

Elizabeth Vandon. Sheed & Ward, 1958.

The Bulletin, November 29, 1958

This is the spiritual autobiography of an artist, now a member of the Catholic Evidence Guild, who was brought up in a materialist atmosphere with only a few depressing religious encounters in her youth. After unsuccessful psychoanalysis for recurrent depression and a near addiction to morphia, she fell into the Church in one of those conversions for which there is no logical explanation except grace.

It is always exciting to read a book of this kind where the reader knows the outcome from the beginning but must wait to learn the means, so often slight or ridiculous, by which the miracle is brought about. This book is not particularly well written, its slanginess is frequently irritating; but it is a true account of the mysterious workings of God in a soul.

reviews and letters

1959

Freud and Religion

Gregory Zilboorg. Newman, 1958.

The Bulletin, January 10, 1959

This, the third of the Woodstock papers edited by Father John Courtney Murray, is a study of Freud's atheism and its sources in his personal life. It is a successful attempt to show that Freud's atheism was not scientific and is not a necessary condition for the practice of psychoanalysis, that Freud's teachings are in fact less dangerous to religion than Jung's theories, which use belief in the practical service of psychotherapy.

Dr. Zilboorg shows that Freud was not a "natural unbeliever" as Dr. Ernest Jones, his friend and biographer, insists. In his insecurity Freud constantly sought faith in unbelief. One of his most persistent interests was the problem and image of Moses, whom he wished to find fully human and historical and Egyptian rather than Jewish, as such a theory would fit in more closely with his own unconscious attitude toward the Hebraic-Christian tradition. Religion was so disturbing emotionally to Freud that he wished to abolish it, and in order to do so, he cut it down to a size "chosen by himself." He made the man in the street the measure of religion. Dr. Zilboorg points out that such a reduction, if applied to science "would make science come off as an art of making mechanical ways."

This is a valuable study for anyone interested in Freudian theories and their compatability with Christian belief.

Temporal and Eternal

Charles Péguy. Harper, 1958.

The Bulletin, January 10, 1959

Apparently it is a great accomplishment to translate Péguy's prose into English. Mauriac once remarked that it was a pity some one didn't translate it into French. The translator in this case, M. Alexander Dru, has been remarkably successful in conveying Péguy's peculiar and powerful rhetoric. He has also contributed a valuable introduction to these two Cahiers which deal with Christianity, or rather with the lack of it, in the modern world, with the progressive transformation of a mystique into a politique, of founders into profiteers, of faith into power.

The first Cahier, "Memories of Youth," is a long essay on the political issues involved in the Dreyfus Affair. Péguy was an ardent Dreyfusite. The second, "Clio I," is a disquisition to the author by the Muse of History, who lays the lack of Christianity in the modern world to the clergy. "It is no riddle. It is no longer a secret, even in the schools, and it can no longer be concealed, except perhaps in the seminaries, that the de-Christianization stems from the clergy. The shrinking, the withering of the trunk of the spiritual city, temporally founded, eternally promised, does not come from the laity, it comes from the clerks." Péguy was in great measure instrumental in decreasing the opposition of liberty and tradition in France. His is a voice which has been listened to to the great benefit of Catholic revival everywhere.

The Nature of Belief

M. C. D'Arcy, S.J. Herder, 1958.

The Bulletin, January 24, 1959

This is a new and revised edition of a study first published in 1931, dealing with the proper grounds for certainty in religious belief. From a very readable first chapter on the present condition of belief, Father D'Arcy proceeds to analyze Newman's *Grammar of Assent*. His critique of Newman's theories of belief is technical and occupies three chapters of reading that will be difficult for anyone who is not a professional student of philosophy and well-acquainted with Newman. In the second part of the book he examines supernatural faith and its relation to desire and love. One chapter, "Empiricism and Certainty," has been added since the 1931 edition, this having been made necessary by those changes in modern thought which have shaken the positivist principle of scientific certainty. This is a valuable book for those who have the time to study it but it will not yield itself readily to the casual reader.

Order and History

Volume 2, *The World of the Polis*
Eric Voegelin. Louisiana State University Press, 1957.

The Bulletin, January 24, 1959

In the first volume of *Order and History*, Eric Voegelin traced the problems of order in Israel from its beginnings with the chosen people through to its climactic symbols of the Suffering Servant and the exodus of Israel from its concrete self.

In Israel this was never a speculative movement; only in Deutero-Isaiah did there appear anything approaching a theoretical treatment of the problem. In the case of Greek order, treated in this second volume of the study, the movement traced is one from myth to speculation. " . . . The society itself, as well as the course of its order, is constituted in retrospect from its end." The Greek experience of order comes finally through its articulation in the symbolic form of philosophy and philosophy arises as a symbol of universally valid order from the orbit of the Greek city-state.

In this volume Voegelin follows the Hellenic consciousness of history as it is motivated by the experience of crisis. Where the Israelite consciousness of history came about by the experience of divine revelation, the Greek came about by the experience of disorder forcing an understanding of order. Voegelin follows this process in Greek culture from the myths of Homer and Hesiod, masterfully analyzed, through to the history of Thucydides who, following Greek medicine, attempted empiricism.

Large sections of this volume will interest only Greek science scholars or professional students of history and political science, but there are other parts, such as those dealing with Homer and Aeschylus, which will be of interest to anyone taking pleasure in literature. "The World of the Polis" leads to the study of Plato and Aristotle with which the third volume will deal.

Religion and the Free Society

Miller, Clancy, Cobsen, Howe, and Kempner. Fund for the Republic.

The Bulletin, February 7, 1959

This pamphlet contains five excellent articles relating to the general issue of religious and civil liberties in the United

States. The authors consistently take a measured and reasoned approach to a subject which is usually argued with thoughtless passion, both by Catholics and by secularists.

William Clancy, in his article, "Religion as a Source of Tension," makes the much needed point that " . . . just as the American government is a voluntary self-limiting government, so the churches, whatever their theological claims are, in terms of their public role in the American society must regard themselves as self-limiting. A Church may be absolutely sure of its own mandate and spiritual authority, yet it cannot publicly act as though that mandate and authority were generally accepted by the civil society. Forms of religious behavior or assertions of religious power that in theological terms may be quite logical and just, or in other societies, in other times and places, might even have been expedient, become dangerously imprudent in the pluralist society that is America." More such statements as this coming from Catholics might tend to curb some of the just suspicion created in the minds of non-Catholics by certain Catholic excesses in social action.

This pamphlet will be sent free of charge to anyone requesting it by the Fund for the Republic, 60 East 42nd Street, New York City 17. It would be well worth any thinking Catholic's time and trouble to send for it.

Harry Vernon at Prep

Franc Smith. Houghton Mifflin, 1959.

The Bulletin, March 7, 1959

This book is an intended satire on prep school teachers. A petty thief with a photographic memory and a good command of academic jargon gets himself a position in an Eastern prep school and in a first person narrative recounts his adventures there. A great comic artist, a Gogol or a Nabokov, might be able to do something with this, but Mr. Smith does not have the qualifications. The book's humor depends entirely on the device of exaggeration, one which appeals mainly to loutish school boys and can be found best exemplified in college humor magazines. If this were the book's only fault it could be recommended for boys who never grow up and dismissed. Unfortunately, it has a pretension to seriousness. The jacket informs us that Mr. Smith attended parochial schools; this is a blinking light to caution the Catholic reader. True to our expectations, the only "good" characters are Catholics, innocent and with hearts of gold. The heel-hero is also basically innocent and with a heart of gold and though he is not a Catholic, he feels a strong attraction to good Catholic living. All this makes a painful book more painful.

Order and History

Volume 3, *Plato and Aristotle*
Eric Voegelin. Louisiana State University Press, 1958.

The Bulletin, May 2, 1959

The larger and more interesting part of this third volume of *Order and History* is devoted to an analysis of Plato's science of order, from the *Republic* through the *Laws*. For Plato society is "man written in larger letters" and therefore the diseases of the soul are carried over into society. Thus the *Republic* begins as a dialogue on the just life of the individual and becomes also an inquiry into order and disorder in society. For Plato, "The philosopher is man in the anxiety of his fall from being; and philosophy is the ascent toward salvation for Everyman. . . . Plato's philosophy, therefore, is not a philosophy but the symbolic form in which a Dionysiac soul expresses its ascent to God." Voegelin makes it clear that the leap in being toward the transcendent source of order is real in Plato but that it stems from the depth of the Dionysiac soul; the prefiguration of the Christian solution is prefiguration only. For Plato the spirit always manifested itself in the visible, finite form of society. He never arrived at the Christian distinction between the temporal and the spiritual.

Plato's enemies were the Sophists and Socrates' arguments against them are still today the classical arguments against that sophistic philosophy of existence which characterizes positivism and the age of enlightenment. These are also Voegelin's enemies; he makes it plain in this volume that the murder of Socrates parallels the political murders of our time.

Christian Asceticism and Modern Man

Edited by Louis Bouyer. Philosophical Library, 1955.

The Bulletin, May 2, 1959

Although this excellent collection of papers on Christian asceticism and the man of today has fourteen authors, it does not lack unity. The papers were contributed by specialists in various fields for a conference organized on the subject by the promoters of *La Vie Spirituelle*. The essays trace ascetic practices from the New Testament through the Renaissance and provide a comprehensive theology of asceticism which maintains its necessity for the full spiritual life. They then proceed to consider the changes in modern life which have made certain of these past means of mortifying the senses both dangerous and dubious for the man of today. Anthropological factors, psychiatric considerations, new knowledge about the relationship between pain and sensuality have all made necessary a change in the application of ascetic devices inherited from the various religious orders.

Whereas the man of the middle ages had exuberance to

control, modern man, living a life of nervous attrition, has little; he "is today a creature divorced from his own nature." Rather than stimulate discipline in himself by sought pain, his need is to gain it through the practice of positive charity. "As the things most unfavorable to the inner life are the insistent presence of an environment tending all the time toward materialism in thought and action, the cult of the self, failure to distinguish between sincerity and truth, fickleness of character and hypersensitiveness of nerves, these are the points against which the ascetic campaign should be directed."

This book is a choice contribution to Catholic intellectual life.

Tell Me, Stranger

Charles B. Flood. Houghton Mifflin, 1959.

The Bulletin, June 27, 1959

In fiction there is nothing worse than the combination of slickness and Catholicism. Whenever problems of faith are dealt with in a novel, the novelist has already committed himself to enter the work at a certain level and to people it with characters more than two dimensional. In this third novel of Charles Brancelen Flood, a young man becomes bored analyzing securities for a Wall Street firm and leaves his job to travel abroad as assistant to a woman photographer. The lady is blonde and divorced; the young man is nothing much but a Catholic. Proximity produces an affair. Although the lady's assets are more immediately appealing than the Church's, the young man gives her up. However, his commendable action appears to stem from the faith of Mr. Flood rather than his own, and this is because he has never come alive as a person. He is depthless and the author doesn't seem to be aware of it. The result, fictionalized apologetics, introduces a depressing new category: light Catholic summer reading.

Light in Silence

Claude Koch. Dodd Mead, 1958.

The Bulletin, July 11, 1959

This is a distinguished, sometimes very funny, occasionally tedious novel, set in a community of brothers on the heights above the Niagara Gorge. Worldly interests and pride of intellect have impinged on what was once a simple mendicant order. The action of the novel is built around the events which restore its original spirit to the Community of St. Bardolph. What is required to get rid of the evil is sanctity and Mr. Koch's portrait of the saint—an old brother known as The Pirate—is both believable and appealing. With great ease he accomplishes one of the most difficult tasks a novelist can set himself. The Pirate, who teaches English and attends condemned movies, disguised in an ancient sweater, embarrasses the "progressive" elements of the community by having a vision during the week when the state examiners are to arrive.

Characters outside of the order are less successfully treated; the book is about a hundred pages too long, but a very fine performance withal.

Nine Sermons of St. Augustine on the Psalms

Translated by Father Edmund Hill. Kenedy, 1959.

The Bulletin, July 25, 1959

Since the American Catholic seldom hears a sermon on any part of the Old Testament, this translation by Father Edmund Hill of nine sermons of St. Augustine on the Psalms should come as a welcome luxury. Unfortunately the sermons have been rendered, in a very free translation, into a prose which is determinedly folksy. St. Augustine, after stating a point, is made to say, "Got it?" Those who can take this, can take anything. The translator informs us that there were many barbarians in St. Augustine's audience and that his Latin was surprisingly conversational. He must therefore have concluded that present day barbarians would delight to hear the great rhetorician say, "Got it?" "off the rails," "inside information," and other such expressions. He apologizes in advance to those readers who find the translation altogether too colloquial. An apology is in order.

The Image Industries

William Lynch, S.J. Sheed & Ward, 1959.

The Bulletin, August 8, 1959

Father Lynch's thesis in this fine book is that the trash put out by the mass media industries is causing the American imagination to rot and that this is as dangerous for the life of the nation as any of the external threats to our security. Fed continuously on a diet of fantasy which is not recognized as such, the American will eventually find his life ordered on a basis of unreality that can destroy the moral fiber of the nation.

It is Father Lynch's contention that in trying to halt this condition we must have the cooperation of artist and theologian, that these two are natural allies. In the last few decades, particularly from Catholic circles, the moral theologian, acting as censor, has been heard from and usually to the detriment of future cooperation with the artist. Fr. Lynch feels that action from the censor will be called for only occasionally, that he must concern himself with what is good workmanship and that he must provide a theology of creativity. "The matter of style is a great theological question, but the theologian, the moralist, and the censor will recognize that it is not their competence, but the competence of art, to destroy the phony, to laugh it out of court, and to create the true. Our task is to encourage them, to raise them up among us, and on our knees beg them to accomplish this task: the task of reality against fantasy."

The World to Come

R. W. Gleason, S.J. Sheed & Ward, 1959.

The Bulletin, August 22, 1959

This is an excellent and needed book on the after-life and one which should serve as an antidote to much popular preaching on the subject. Medieval thought on the world to come was concerned with the elaboration of a theology of the states after death and at times, as the author points out, devoted attention to questions more curious than decisive. In the 16th century, the emphasis took on the polemic and apologetic tone of the times, made necessary by the Counter-Reformation.

In modern times, the theologian is interested in the idea

of death on more speculative grounds. He wishes to use all the intellectual discoveries of contemporary thought, regardless of their source, to illuminate the subject for modern man whose concerns are increasingly existential and personalistic rather than curious or apologetic. Father Gleason succeeds admirably in doing this particularly in his chapters on Hell, Redemptive Suffering, and the Resurrection.

The treatment of Purgatory is especially illuminating. "The medieval mind, avid as it was of mystical visions and particularly preoccupied with the state of the dead, was over-rich in 'revelations' concerning purgatory. These detailed descriptions, which create horror in the modern mind, are not to be taken as Christian doctrine." Father Gleason presents Purgatory as a possibility for interior development. This book will be welcomed by anyone who feels the need of a fresh intellectual approach to the subject.

Faith and Understanding in America

Gustave Weigel, S.J. Macmillan, 1959.

The Bulletin, August 22, 1959

The Catholic who wishes to understand the intellectual problems of his time cannot afford to be ignorant of modern Protestant theology, which only in specific cases, bears much resemblance to the doctrines of the original reformers. Increasingly what is happening to Protestant thought is of concern to Catholics and some of the best (and with obvious limitations, most sympathetic) commentaries available on the subject are by Catholics, such as Fathers Weigel, D'Arcy, and Tavard.

In *Faith and Understanding in America* Father Weigel takes advantage of the growing possibility of communication between Catholics and Protestants in this country to point out some of the problems, limits and advantages of Catholic participation in ecumenical movements. His discussion of the split in Protestant theology ranges from a consideration of the truly great writings of Barth to the popular absurdities of Dr. Norman Vincent Peale ("Prayerize, Picturize, Actualize!"). He points out that Catholics, while neither fundamentalists nor liberals are doctrinally closer to Protestant fundamentals than to those liberal Protestant theologians who have created a naturalistic ethical culture, humanism, and labeled it Christianity. This, although Father Weigel does not mention it, is of particular interest to the Catholic in the South when he considers his possible contribution to Southern life in the future. It is an embarrassment to our fundamentalist neighbors to realize that they are doctrinally nearer their traditional enemy, the Church of Rome, than they are to modern Protestantism. The day may come when Catholics will be the ones who maintain the spiritual traditions of the South.

Father Weigel's book should be given careful attention by all of us.

Zen and Japanese Culture

Bollingen Series 64, Second Edition
D. T. Suzuki. Pantheon, 1959.

The Bulletin, October 17, 1959

Unlike other forms of Buddhism which have influenced the spiritual life mainly, Zen has influenced every phase of the cultural life of Japan. Mr. Suzuki traces its influence in swordsmanship, the art of tea, the Japanese love of nature, and in Japanese poetry, particularly haiku, the seventeen syllable verse form very popular in Japan. Zen has impinged on the American consciousness lately by way of highly vocal Bohemian groups found currently in San Francisco and other large cities. These people, in their revolt from our exaggerated materialist values, turn more often to Zen than to Christianity.

The Catholic reading Mr. Suzuki's book will be interested in deducing from it reasons for this. Zen, although it teaches poverty and charity and ethically bears a superficial resemblance to Christianity, is non-conceptual, non-purposive, and non-historical, and therefore admirably suited to be exploited by the non-thinker and pseudo-artist. It seems to have blended over the centuries with the Japanese character to produce delicate art forms such as haiku. Its insights are genuine but not suited to a vigorous art. It can combine itself readily with many cultures, philosophies and theologies, but hardly with orthodox Christianity. One of Mr. Suzuki's best illustrations of the incompatability of Zen and Christianity is his comparison of the death scenes of Christ and the Buddha—Christ, vertical in agony against the cross, the Buddha contentedly falling asleep on his couch.

Rosmini

Claude Leetham. Helicon, 1958.

The Bulletin, November 14, 1959

Antonio Rosmini, philosopher, statesman and priest, founder of the Institute of Charity, was one of the great churchmen of the 19th century. The causes he spoke for then read like a catalogue of improvements that have eventually come to pass in the Church in the 20th century or in some cases of matters that are still in agitation. He favored the revival of the philosophy of St. Thomas, the use of the vernacular in the liturgy, the necessity for an understanding of Eastern philosophies, and native clergy. His political philosophy was substantially that of Leo XIII but preceded it by half a century and was regarded in its time as dangerous and unrealistic. He was viciously persecuted by high churchmen who, according to G. Bozzetti who provides the introduction, "thus transformed his testimony into acute martyrdom."

More than with his philosophical or political accomplishments the reader of this biography will be impressed with Rosmini's balanced good sense in guiding the Institute of Charity. He seems to have had the only clear head in the Institute. Its members were the first missionaries to the English in the 19th century and some of the most interesting parts of this book deal with Rosmini's difficulty in controlling by correspondence their Italian excesses in devotion. He was continually having to restrain them from forcing scapulars and rigorous retreats on the English instead of instilling in them devotion to the essentials of the religion, or what he called the "bread" of the faith rather than the "sugar." This is a rewarding biography of a man full of good sense.

The Devil's Advocate

Morris L. West. Morrow, 1959.

The Bulletin, December 12, 1959

The Devil's Advocate is a swiftly moving novel concerned with a priest's return to spiritual reality in the last few months of his life. Msgr. Meridith, dying of cancer, is sent to a small Italian mountain village to investigate for beatification a man murdered fourteen years before by Communist partisans. In the course of his investigation, he learns to care for souls, to become a pastor in the real sense, and to meet death in the act of trying to save another. Parallel to this interest is the investigation itself and the question of the supposed saint and his possible sanctity. This latter line of action makes of the book a kind of mystery novel and undoubtedly accounts for its presence on the best seller list. The best seller list is a standard of mediocrity through which occasionally a work of merit will slip for reasons unconnected with its quality. In spite of a style which is more frequently deft than distinguished, *The Devil's Advocate* is a work of merit.

It is also what can safely be called a Catholic novel, being both explicitly concerned with a certain aspect of the life of the Church, and implicitly directed by Catholic belief. As a novel it is a curious blend of slickness and profundity. It is almost as if a very good and a mediocre novel had been stitched together with a jagged line to make one book. The investigating priest is always believable, the investigated candidate for beatification almost never so. This book is well worth reading for its virtues and we have its faults to thank for its being read so widely.

Religion and the Psychology of Jung

Raymond Hostie. Translated by G. R. Lamb. Sheed & Ward, 1959.

Unpublished Review

The psychology of Jung is of particular interest to Catholics because Jung, breaking with Freud sometime after 1913, was the first modern psychologist to put forward ideas arising from the relationship of analytical psychology and religion. Fr. Hostie, a Belgian Jesuit priest who has attended the Jung Institute in Zurich, thoroughly and competently examines

Jung's empirical method and fundamental ideas and compares them with his religious ideas, always making the necessary distinctions between the psychological and the ontological aspects of religion.

While Fr. Hostie is able to agree with many of Jung's conclusions, he points out that psychology can tell us nothing about metaphysics or theology in themselves or about God, their specific object. He says, "Jung's contribution to philosophy, theology and religion remains . . . indirect. I have acknowledged his right to enter this field . . . but he in his turn should be prepared to accept the limitations which his science imposes upon him."

This is a thorough and valuable book for anyone interested in analytical psychology or for anyone interested in the problems that the church has to face in combatting a growing attitude which tends toward psychologism in its appraisal of religion.

reviews and letters

1960

Jesus Christus

Romano Guardini. Regnery, 1959.

Mary, Mother of Faith

Josef Weiger. Regnery, 1959.

The Bulletin, February 6, 1960

Jesus Christus is a short book of meditations on the life of Christ, originally delivered as sermons to the students at Berlin University when Monsignor Guardini was preparing to write his major work, *The Lord*. This book is only a sample of what is brought to fruition in *The Lord*. Perhaps it has been offered for those who would be frightened of a larger book. Any sample of Monsignor Guardini's religious spirit can be gratefully received if it leads readers to his major work.

Mary, Mother of Faith is a longer book of meditations on the life of the Virgin. Monsignor Guardini who contributes the introduction, points out that there is "a way of speaking of Mary which presupposes that honour is proportionate to the abandon with which one encomium is piled upon another," and that this tendency is responsible for the aversion that many feel at the mention of Mary. This book avoids the treacly and exaggerated presentations that we are accustomed to receive in sermons and considers the Mother of God largely in relation to the virtue of faith and its absolute necessity in her life. It is a quiet and simple work but repetitious and not as intellectually stimulating as Jean Guitton's book on the Virgin.

The Phenomenon of Man

Pierre Teilhard de Chardin. Harper, 1959.

Pierre Teilhard de Chardin

Claude Tresmontant. Helicon, 1959.

The Bulletin, February 20, 1960

In a recent review of *The Phenomenon of Man*, *The London Times Literary Supplement* says, "There have been men hardly recognized in their lifetime for whose acquaintance later generations would willingly have sacrificed much." The name of Pierre Teilhard de Chardin, to whom the *Times* referred, is so little known in America that in his introduction to Claude Tresmontant's study of Pierre Teilhard's thought, Fr. Gustave Weigel regards it as not an impertinence to tell us how to pronounce his name: Tay-ahr. It is a name which future generations will know better than we do.

Pierre Teilhard was a Jesuit and a paleontologist. *The Phenomenon of Man* is a work on evolution in which human life is seen as converging toward a point which Pierre Teilhard calls Omega and which he identified with Christ. Although Teilhard was allowed to continue his scientific work, the book was not allowed by his superiors to be published in his lifetime. It was completed in 1938 and published in 1959 by the friends to whom Teilhard left it. Only a man of profound Catholic piety could have sustained his love for the Church and his order under these circumstances, but Teilhard was a great Christian; his vision of Christ was as real as his love for science; his mind dealt in immensities.

This is a work which makes demands on the scientist, the theologian and the poet. Its scientific value is vouched for by Sir Julian Huxley, who contributes an introduction in which he says that Père Teilhard has effected "a threefold synthesis—of the material and physical world with the world of mind and spirit; of the past with the future; and of variety with unity, the many with the one" and that the measure of his stature is that he so largely succeeded in the search for human significance in the evolutionary process. Huxley, of course, regards Teilhard's linking of Christianity with evolution as merely a "gallant attempt," but we could not expect him to go further.

The theological aspects of Teilhard's work are ably and sympathetically discussed by Claude Tresmontant in his book, *Pierre Teilhard de Chardin: His Thought*. Tresmontant, while admitting Teilhard was not a good metaphysician, vigorously defends his orthodoxy. It is fortunate that the two books have been published at the same time in this country, for the critical book gives an insight into the real greatness of Teilhard and definitively sets out his contribution to Christian spirituality. In his early years Teilhard was oppressed by a caricature of Christianity, one to a large degree prevalent today in American Catholic life, which sees human perfection as consisting in escape from the world and from nature. Nature in this light is seen as already fulfilled. Teilhard, rediscovering biblical thought, "asserts that creation is still in full gestation and that the duty of the Christian is to cooperate with it." Humanity, Teilhard wrote, "is very far from being fully created, neither in its individual developments nor, above all, in the collective terminus toward which it is directed. . . ." Tresmontant points out that asceticism in Teilhard's view no longer "consists so much in liberating and purifying oneself from 'matter'—but in further spiritualizing matter . . . in sanctifying and supernaturalizing the real which has been given to us, by 'working together' with God." Actually Teilhard's work is a scientific rediscovery of St. Paul's thought.

Because Teilhard is both a man of science and a believer, the scientist and the theologian will perhaps require a long time to sift his thought and accept it, but the poet, whose sight is essentially prophetic, will at once recognize in this immense vision his own. Teilhard believed that what the world needs now is a new way to sanctity. His way, that of spiritualizing matter, is actually a very old way, one which throughout history is always being obscured by one form of heresy or another. It is the path which the artist has always taken to his particular goals, but which is set before our minds now in a scientific expression. *The Phenomenon of Man* is a work which should bring the worlds of science, of art, and of theology closer toward that convergence which Père Teilhard saw as their luminous destiny.

Editor's Note: Flannery O'Connor also reviewed *The Phenomenon of Man* in the Fall 1961 issue of *The American Scholar*. See p. 129.

Sister Clare

Loretta Burrough. Houghton Mifflin, 1960.

The Pyx

John Buell. Farrar, Straus & Cudahy, 1959.

The Bulletin, April 16, 1960

Sister Clare will possibly be admired by those who are tired of novels in which nuns decide that convent life is not for them. The nun in this novel does not question her vocation. Her trials are with commonplaces such as washing down the belfry stairs and with a pride which is exhibited several times and is considered by her superiors a great impediment to Carmelite perfection. Most of the nuns in this book who do not have lovably tart tongues speak with a pious coyness which may, unfortunately, be authentic. The note of the novel is authenticity to Carmelite life; it is not depth of characterization. Any novel which seeks to do justice to a religious vocation, and particularly one to the severe order of Mt. Carmel, will have to go very deeply into the inner life of its main character, and this is perhaps an impossibility in the case of mystics of this kind. The book may be of interest to girls from twelve to twenty who want to know what life is like in such a convent, but the world of near-perfection seldom makes good fiction.

At the other extreme is *The Pyx*, which should be kept away from children twelve to twenty, although it is the better-written novel. It deals with a milieu almost entirely evil in which, nevertheless, martyrs may be found. The martyr in this case is a prostitute who, when she is about to be forced into participation in something like a black mass, swallows the host which has been given her to desecrate and for this is thrown off a balcony to her death. The book proceeds like a mystery novel but is also a mystery novel in the sense of leaving the reader with a deeper mystery to ponder when the literal mystery has been solved. The evil in this novel is as rarified as the good in *Sister Clare*. Both books follow their own logic but neither quite gets away with it.

God's Frontier

J. L. M. Descalzo, S.J. Knopf, 1959.

The Bulletin, May 14, 1960

The most interesting part of *God's Frontier* is the short introduction by its Jesuit author in which he reminds us that edifying literature is made with heavy "blocks of stone and painful blows of the pick." A translator's note informs the reader that in Spanish the word edification has not lost the meaning of "act of building, of raising an edifice." The author reminds us that edifying literature can only be the work of mature beings and asks if he shall be blamed if some of the pages of his work bleed or sizzle.

Unfortunately, none of them do bleed or sizzle. There is an excellent mind behind this book but it is not the mind of a novelist. The story is of a young man who finds that he works miracles without wanting to—embarrassing miracles, such as bringing a canary back to life when the miracle the community wants is rain to alleviate a persistent drought. This makes good allegory but genuine edification in the sense defined is lacking because there are not enough blows of the axe, very little even of the spade work required to make fiction. The characters remain too easily good or bad, too puppet-like to sustain belief in them for long. Allegory is all that remains and edification in the less interesting, diluted and abstract sense.

This novel won the Eugenio Nadal Prize in Spain, which indicates that it must have had something in Spanish that it lacks in English—perhaps a poetic quality—or that there was no better novel to choose from, or that critical literary values were not uppermost in the minds of the judges.

The Modernity of St. Augustine

Jean Guitton. Helicon, 1959.

The Bulletin, May 14, 1960

This is a brief but illuminating essay on the relevance of St. Augustine to the modern age, particularly as regards his conception of existence in time. Before Augustine the sense of personal sin and its connection with time had had no literary expression. For the Greek, sin was error; for the Stoic accident. The Jews had experienced sin and its relation to history collectively but St. Augustine is the first man of the West to have attained in personal fashion this Jewish experience and to have written it for the ages. M. Guitton traces aspects of Augustinian thought in Freud, Sartre, Proust, Gide and Hegel, indicating the further step into profundity that the saint took which these modern thinkers stop short of. This essay was delivered in Paris on the 16th centenary of St. Augustine's birth and in Geneva before the Faculty of Protestant Theology. It is full of profound suggestions which deserve extension into a longer book.

Letter to Eileen Hall, June 2, 1960

I'm real sorry the book section of The Bulletin *will be discontinued, as it was certainly the most intelligent thing they had in the paper, which is pedestrian otherwise. Somebody owes you a big vote of thanks but I doubt if you'll get it. Anyway, I'm glad of the good library job and I hope you'll enjoy it.*

I have three books that I'm due you reports on, but I'll take The Science of the Cross *if nobody else wants it. It will take me a little time to get these I have read and the reports written.*

Is there any chance of somebody else taking over the book column, or do the editors have a complete disinterest in books?

Letter to "A," July 23, 1960

According to Eileen, Mr. Zuber has written offering himself for the book column, so I reckon we will plug along. A man probably won't have the time or patience to fool with it long, but we shall see.

The Christian Message and Myth

L. Malevz, S.J. Newman, 1958.

The Bulletin, July 23, 1960

This is a critique of the theory of Rudolph Bultmann, one of the most interesting of the new Protestant theologians. Bultmann's concern is to make a real Christianity acceptable to the man of the modern world—real Christianity as distinct from that purely liberal Protestantism that eventually ends in a system of ethical values, but not real Christianity as the orthodox know it. Bultmann wishes to preserve the central Christian message of the cross but to take away everything unacceptable to modern science, thus discarding every intervention of the Divine into human life. He calls this demythologization. He would judge the Christian message as found in the gospels by its relevance to an existential philosophy.

Fr. Malevz throws considerable light on this attempt in an appendix which compares the opposed conceptions of Biblical exegesis and philosophy of Bultmann and Barth. While he favors the conception of Bultmann, he deplores the poverty of his metaphysic. This will be an enlightening and clarifying book for the growing number of Catholics who are interested in knowing more about Protestant theology as it is today rather than as it was in the 15th century.

Letter to Eileen Hall, August 1960

This is a very nice letter from Mr. Markwalter and I am glad that he realizes what you have done. I hope Mr. Zuber takes the thing over. Please tell him I'll do anything I can to help him if he does. . . . I haven't seen any books that I want to review but if I do I'll try writing off for them. You seem to have enough to last for a while.*

*John E. Markwalter, editor of *The Southern Cross*, a publication of the Diocese of Savannah.

Letter to Leo J. Zuber, August 3, 1960

A card from Mrs. Hall says you are going to take over editing the book section in the Bulletin. *I am mighty glad you are and I hope it won't prove a nuisance. I enclose a review which I presume I am now supposed to send to you. I have one more to go after this one.*

Mrs. Hall said you'd request books for us. If nobody else wants it, I'd like to have Modern Catholic Thinkers, *ed. A. R. Caponigri, Harper and Brothers, NYC 16. I have often wondered why Mrs. Hall didn't have the publishers send the book directly to the person she wanted to review it. I have had a mental picture of her spending her life on the way to and from the post office.*

If I can be of any help, please call on me.

Christ and Apollo

William F. Lynch, S.J. Sheed & Ward, 1960.

The Bulletin, August 20, 1960

In *Christ and Apollo*, Fr. Lynch describes the true nature of the literary imagination as founded on a penetration of the finite and limited. The opposition here is between Christ, Who stands for reality in all its definiteness, and Apollo, who stands for the indefinite, the romantic, the endless. It is again the opposition between the Hebraic imagination, always concrete, and the agnostic imagination, which is dream-like. In genuine tragedy and comedy, the definite is explored to its extremity and man is shown to be the limited creature he is, and it is at this point of greatest penetration of the limited that the artist finds insight. Much modern so-called tragedy avoids this penetration and makes a leap toward transcendence, resulting in an unearned and spacious resolution of the work. The principle of this thorough penetration of the limited is best exemplified in medieval scriptural exegesis, in which three kinds of meaning were found in the literal level of the sacred text: the moral, the allegorical, and the anagogical. This is the Catholic way of reading nature as well as scripture, and it is a way which leaves open the most possibilities to be found in the actual.

If Fr. Lynch's book could have a wide Catholic audience in this country, particularly in the colleges, it might ultimately help in the formidable task of raising our level of literary appreciation.

Letter to Leo J. Zuber, August 30, 1960

My mother and I would be delighted to have you come down and bring your wife and what children are not being sat with, and spend the afternoon with us some time before it gets cold. I suggest the latter part of September when the leaves have begun to turn. The drive down then would be pleasanter than now. Let us know when to expect you.

I know [someone else] will take The Leopard *off your hands and save me from that penitential duty.*

I'd like to see the list; there is also a book I'd like to review if no one else wants to: Soul and Psyche, *Victor White, O.P., Harper & Bros.*

When you come down, you will find us on Highway 441, 16 miles from Eatonton and 4 miles before you come to Milledgeville, on the right hand side of the road, a two-story white farm house. Fr. Paul at the monastery can tell you where if you happen to see him. He is our mutual friend. He and my mother consult each other upon gardening.

The Son of Man

François Mauriac. World, 1960.

The Bulletin, September 3, 1960

M. Mauriac's meditation on Christ reveals, as might be expected on any man's meditation on the Lord, a good deal more about himself than about Christ. One comes away from this book impressed afresh with Mauriac's sense of Christ's presence in the contemporary world, but remembering perhaps longer certain pictures of Mauriac as a child, his feet sweating in his cold shoes as he waits on a freezing morning to go to school. This is a novelist's meditation; Mauriac is always able to impress the reader with a strong sense of the flesh—all men's flesh that Christ takes on—and of the anguish of the human situation. In this book he provides a specific answer for the Jansenism of which he has often been accused.

He proposes in the place of that anguish that Gide called the Catholic's "cramp of salvation,"—obsession with personal salvation—an anguish transmuted into charity, anguish for another. Thus for Sartre, "hell is other people," but for the Christian with Mauriac's anguish others are Christ. We realize that this way of looking at life was so completely left out of Mauriac's youthful Catholic education that it has had to come to him as a discovery of later life. This is a valuable book, one which will provide the reader with unforeseen insights into the Incarnation.

Letter to "A," September 17, 1960

I'm glad Mr. Zuber has come forth. He must be mighty sociable as he has already indicated he and his wife would like to come down and spend the afternoon, a proposal I find very agreeable as I would like to get a look at him myself.

The Science of the Cross

Edith Stein. Regnery, 1960.

The Bulletin, October 1, 1960

This book is a presentation of the life and doctrine of St. John of the Cross by Edith Stein, a Jewish Carmelite nun who met her death in the gas chambers at Auschwitz. It is her last work and knowing the outcome of her life, one feels in it the modern fulfillment of St. John's doctrine by herself.

As for St. John of the Cross, his life was lived so very near eternal realities that it seems an impossible life to understand. One must simply accept it on faith with no recourse to psychology. Edith Stein was at one time the disciple of the phenomenologist, Edmund Husserl. Her intellectual training was not in theology but in philosophy of the phenomenologist school. Both the translator and the editor of this book point out that this background makes a difference in Edith Stein's approach to St. John, but the reader who looks for the difference will perhaps find it in very few instances. The book seems largely made up of quotations from St. John which Edith Stein adds very little to. It is a moving book but less for what is in it than for Edith Stein's own background—for the modern crucifixion that the reader knows was waiting for her as she wrote the book.

Beat on a Damask Drum

T. K. Martin. Dutton, 1960.

The Bulletin, October 1, 1960

This is a very well-written war novel with religious undertones. It traces the penetration into reality of a film actress who insinuates herself into the hide-out of five soldiers of fortune in French Indo China. Her intention is to retrieve one of them, a childhood companion, and bring him back to London to live her kind of life, a kind of life which he and all those who have experienced the horror of modern war and the precariousness of modern life have out-grown. In the process of trying to get him back, she learns the lesson of Christ's final abandonment on the cross. Occasionally meaning in this book is lost in shadows and credibility strained, but in general it is a novel well worth reading once and possibly twice.

Letter to Leo J. Zuber, October 4, 1960

The 18th would be fine except that I am going to be in Minnesota. I have to talk at two Catholic colleges, one in Winona and one in St. Paul. I would say the week after that but that week I am going to be tied up with the Wesleyan Arts Festival. What about the first or second week in November? Time gets away from me. I hadn't realized this Minnesota thing was right on me.

There is a girl in Savannah named Mary Harty (Miss) who did some reviewing for Mrs. Hall but I haven't seen her name or anything in a long time. I don't have her address though she is a cousin of mine, but I think she might like to start reviewing again. I think she has been in Europe. You could get her address from Mrs. Hall. She's the only one I can think of off hand, but I will keep thinking. Oh. There is a Sister Alice at the Cancer Home in Atlanta who writes and might like to do some reviewing (simple things).

Letter to Leo J. Zuber, October 12, 1960

Just so I get Soul & Psyche *eventually—*

I returned the Image & Idea *as I think the people who want them ought to have them.*

I don't guess I'll run into Fr. Barry as I am supposed to be going to Winona and St. Paul, but I appreciate your mentioning my visit to him.

Pierre Teilhard de Chardin

Nicolas Corte. Macmillan, 1960.

The Bulletin, October 15, 1960

Until Claude Cuenot's definitive biography of Teilhard is published in this country, this long essay on the noted evolutionist's life and spirit will have to fill a place for which it is an inadequate but interesting stop-gap. Nicolas Corte is the pseudonym of a French Monsignor, a professor emeritus at one of the French universities. The biographical part of the book is hardly more than a matter of he-went-here, then-he-went-there, and is considerably less interesting than the even shorter biographical section in Claude Tresmontant's book on Teilhard. In an introduction, the translator, Martin Jarret-Kerr, C.R., remarks that Corte hardly does justice to Teilhard's loyalty to the Church, an aspect of the Jesuit's life that his non-Catholic admirers find hard to understand or take, though it is the fact about Teilhard that is the key to his personality. Nicolas Corte, while admiring it, takes it for granted as almost any Catholic would.

The more interesting part of the book is taken up with Corte's assembling and outlining the main critical objection both from theologians and scientists on Teilhard's thought. This too is inadequate but balanced. In an interesting evaluation at the end of the book, Corte compares Teilhard—whom some have compared to Aquinas since he wished to reconcile the new learning with the old—not to St. Thomas but to Origen. This comparison, like the book as a whole, is suggestive and in the end may prove to be just, but more thorough study will be required to indicate the depth of Teilhard's life and spirit.

Soul and Psyche

Victor White, O.P. Harper, 1960.

The Bulletin, October 29, 1960

Subtitled "An enquiry into the relationship of psychiatry and religion," this book explores more thoroughly some of the same ground that Fr. White surveyed in *God and the Unconscious*. His main object in this study is to show that the conception of a separation of soul and psyche is untenable from the standpoint of both pastor and psychiatrist. This is a proposition hotly denied by a great many eminent psychiatrists and theologians. Whether Fr. White convinces the reader of his point or not, he will at least deepen his understanding of the relationship between the two.

Some of the most interesting parts of the book are hints thrown off in passing which show that attention to the study of archetypes could benefit the Church in some of the acute pastoral problems she faces today. In discussing the prevalent lapse of Catholics brought up in Catholic homes and educated in Catholic schools, Fr. White observes that this is very likely a failure of our sacred images to sustain an adequate idea of what they are supposed to represent. The images absorbed in childhood are retained by the soul throughout life. In medieval times, the child viewed the same images as his elders, and these were images adequate to the realities they stood for. He formed his images of the Lord from, for example, the stern and majestic Pantacrator, not from a smiling Jesus with a bleeding heart. When childhood was over, the image was still valid and was able to hold up under the assaults given to belief. Today the idea of religion of large numbers of Catholics remains trapped at the magical stage by static and superficial images which neither mind nor stomach can any longer take.

This discussion alone makes *Soul and Psyche* worth reading.

Christian Initiation

Louis Bouyer. Macmillan, 1960.

The Bulletin, November 12, 1960

This very short book is a restatement of religious truth, beginning with first perceptions of the spiritual and continuing through the discovery of God, of the Divine Word, of the living Church and the Eucharist, and finally of eternal life. It is intended to show the reader how faith takes root in the intelligence, but it is perhaps too summary a book to do this successfully.

Louis Bouyer is one of the most interesting theologians writing today. This particular work, however, has the quality of an exercise. It lacks the excitement of Fr. Bouyer's other well-known works, "The Spirit and Forms of Protestantism," and his biography of Newman. In a short introduction, the author says that it is a book written not so much to read as to reread. It is possibly a book best suited to furnish the basis of meditations on the Christian mystery.

Letter to Leo J. Zuber, November 26, 1960

We certainly enjoyed the visit and want you all to come again.

I'll write Cross Currents *and ask them about the same thing* you asked the people at* Jubilee. *They might give me some information about the magazine that would be good to include.*

The books I have that I'll review are The Divine Milieu *and* Catholics in Conversation.

I asked the Sister Superior at the Cancer Home about the presses of religious orders and she threw up her hands and said, "As a last resort, as a last resort!" So we'll try everything else first.

I have hopes for the book page of the Bulletin *now.*

*This refers to a book by the Dominican Nuns of Our Lady of Perpetual Help Home (for children with cancer, in Atlanta, Georgia), *A Memoir of Mary Ann*. O'Connor wrote an introduction and helped the nuns to find a publisher (Farrar, Straus, and Cudahy, 1961).

Letter to Leo J. Zuber, December 10, 1960

I enclose the review of Catholics in Conversation.

This is an interesting letter from Mr. Cunneen. He appears to be tired and worn out, but I think it would be wonderful to have him send in some summaries of articles in Catholic magazines—even if it were only from articles in Cross Currents. *If you want me to do the article on* Cross Currents, *I won't be able to until after Christmas as I am entering Piedmont Hospital next Tuesday to have my bones inspected. I hope I won't be there long, but the trip will kill at least a week.*

Letter to Leo J. Zuber, December 18, 1960

Thanks for your letter and for the ad about the MacLeish book. I am not much on MacLeish so I'll let that one go. I'll do the Cross Currents *one next but I want to write poor Cunneen myself first.*

Incidentally, a girl who works at Lippincott sent me that Catholics in Conversation *free, so you had better temper your wrath when you send them the review. The Teilhard I bought meself as when Mrs. H. asked for* The Phenomenon of Man *they wouldn't send it.*

A most happy Christmas to you both.

Modern Catholic Thinkers

Edited by A. Robert Caponigri. Harper, 1960.

The Bulletin, December 24, 1960

To anyone who happens to be skeptical about the modern Catholic's freedom and ability to contribute to the intellectual life of our times, this book should be presented. In his introduction, Fr. D'Arcy, S.J., notes that those who are prejudiced against Catholic thinkers "count it against them that their views are very old and musty. The art of living and thinking, they claim, is to be contemporary. Furthermore, not only are the ideas they follow out of date; they are bound to accept an authorized version and therefore, to repeat a lesson by heart. The Catholic is as tied to a set of formulas as the Marxist; he is equally intransigent and with a mind closed to other ideas. Such critics are inclined to look upon counter-arguments as special pleading."

Dr. Caponigri, assuming that evidence to the contrary is the only suitable method of persuading such dissenting critics, has brought together thirty-eight essays by Catholics whose work leaves no suspicion that any system of ideas has been imposed or true liberty of thought curtailed. Aside from the excellence of Dr. Caponigri's choices, the anthology has the further advantage of leading the reader to the original work from which many of these essays have been taken, and in presenting him with translations of significant chapters of books which have not and may never be published in this country. The selections range from a chapter, "Human and Divine," taken from the well-known *Mind and Heart of Love* by Fr. D'Arcy, to "Existentialism," from an unpublished manuscript of Regis Jolivet.

This anthology will make an excellent Christmas gift for any college student brighter than most or for anyone else concerned with the life of the mind.

reviews and letters

1961

Letter to "A," January 21, 1961

I asked Leo (I still address him Mr. Zuber as he still addresses me Miss O'Connor) to get me Guardini's book on St. Augustine, whereupon he sent me everything on St. Augustine he had in stock and ordered me the one I wanted too.

Letter to Leo J. Zuber, January 23, 1961

Thought you would like to know that Farrar, Straus and Cudahy are going to publish the book that the sisters at the Cancer Home have written about Mary Ann. We are saved from the Daughters of St. Paul! Jubilee *will print the introduction in its April issue and announce the book.*

The Divine Milieu

Pierre Teilhard de Chardin. Harper, 1960.

The Bulletin, February 4, 1961

"Where is the Catholic as passionately vowed (by conviction and not by convention) to spreading the hopes of the Incarnation as are many humanitarians to spreading the dream of the new city?" Teilhard asks this question toward the end of *The Divine Milieu*, the second of his books to be published in America. It is a question depressing to answer today when the sense of expectation has largely disappeared from our religion. No writer of the last few centuries is more capable of restoring that sense to the Christian world than Teilhard, whose work is both scientific and profoundly Pauline.

Teilhard, who was a Jesuit and a paleontologist, was not allowed by his order to publish but was permitted to continue his work and was sent to China, the best place for its continuance. There he played a major role in the discovery of Pekin man and wrote the books which are being published now after his death and which will probably have the effect of giving a new face to Christian spirituality. The first of Teilhard's books to be published here, *The Phenomenon of Man*, is scientific and traces the development of man through the chemical, biological and reflective stages of life. This second volume is religious and puts the first in proper focus. They should be read together for the first volume is liable to seem heretical without the second and the second insubstantial without the first. It is doubtful if any Christian of this century can be fully aware of his religion until he has reseen it in the cosmic light which Teilhard has cast upon it.

Letter to William Sessions,* February 8, 1961

I thank you for the Guardini and will relish it when it arrives. Mr. Zuber couldn't get it for me. Mr. Zuber is doing his best to revolutionize the Bulletin, *beginning with the book section. I pale before his energy. If you want to do some reviews, I am sure he would like to have you.*

*Professor of English at Georgia State University.

Letter to Leo J. Zuber, February 17, 1961

Enclose the Gilson-etta. That was crafty of you to get us insinuated into the back page of the Critic. *As for the* Bulletin *and the book page, the tail will soon be wagging the dog.*

Glad to hear Giroux thinks the book will be of interest to readers over the country. I have my doubts but then I never thought it would get published in the first place. In fact, I bet the Sisters a pair of peafowl nobody would buy it. They are coming down next week to collect their winnings.*

* *A Memoir of Mary Ann.*

Letter to Leo J. Zuber, February 19, 1961

Very crafty of you to send the penitential list at the last two weeks of lent. I have numbered four, in the order of horror, that you may get rid of on me.

Letter to Leo J. Zuber, Spring 1961

Three down and old Benét to go. The two short ones I thought were too short for the bylines so I put initials like they do in Jubilee.

Thanks for the letter of Miss Betty, a reader in New Jersey.

Could you get me a novel called "Judgment of the Sea" by Gertrud von Le Fort, Regnery Chicago?

Why don't you all come down and see us again now that the weather is getting decent?

Catholics in Conversation

Donald McDonald. Lippincott, 1960.

The Bulletin, March 4, 1961

In this lively book, Mr. McDonald interviews seventeen prominent Catholics on subjects relating to Catholic life in the United States and their own contribution to it. The interview is an unnatural form of conversation and is made more so by the presence of the tape recorder, but Mr. McDonald has managed to get the most out of the people he has interviewed. This may be because they have been chosen by himself and their opinions and interests are largely compatible with his own. Those interviewed are Catholics of a markedly liberal viewpoint such as John Cogley, Dorothy Day, and Senator Eugene J. McCarthy. It would be interesting to compile another list of people—a more varied, recalcitrant, and less edifying mixture—for Mr. McDonald to cope with in another book.

Catholics in Conversation could, with value to all, be an annual volume.

Edmund Fuller, in the *New York Times* Book Section, suggested that the interviews could well have been selected to be of more interest to Protestants. There is a case to be made out for the view that the Protestant will be equally, if not more, fascinated to read the interviews with people whose concerns are confined to life within the Church, such as the one with Sister Emil on the Sister Formation Movement or that with the Rev. Alfred Longley, a Minnesota pastor. These take them very effectively "inside" Catholic problems.

Whatever the Protestant may find of value here, it is certain that the Catholic will find a great deal. Most Catholics don't know what is going on in the Church anyhow, and the best way to begin to show them seems to be through personalities rather than abstractions.

The Life of St. Catherine of Siena

Raymond of Capua. Kenedy, 1960.

The Bulletin, March 18, 1961

The signs and wonders that increased the faith of the 14th century will very generally have the opposite effect on that of the 20th, and this biography of St. Catherine, written by her confessor, Blessed Raymond of Capua, can very well have the effect of inspiring the reader with a genuine repulsion for the saint. For many of the miracles herein described, we can find natural causes, others we can ascribe to the imagination, and some to the gullibility of the author, but when the reader has cut down these things to manageable proportions, there still remains the hard core of Catherine's sanctity to be mined out of Blessed Raymond's tiresome platitudes and preaching.

Catherine was a non-conformist of a high order and had all the stubbornness necessary to carry out her way of life. The consternation of her family at finding themselves with a visionary in the house, a daughter who scourged herself three times a day until the blood ran, ate nothing but herbs, and occasionally fell in the fire during her ecstasies (but was never burned) is well detailed by Blessed Raymond. What emerges most profoundly is that all the saint's actions were conformed to a Reality of which the ordinary man is not aware. If the reader can once realize the strength and power of Catherine's vision, the scourgings and other self-punishments become understandable. Conversely, it is only from these penances that the vision can be surmised and vouched for. Altogether this is not a book to give anyone faith, but one which only faith can make understandable.

Letter to Leo J. Zuber, Spring 1961

This takes care of old Benét. Now to the mystics.

Thanks for the picture of all the little Zubers. You must bring them all so we can meet them in person.

I hope Msgr. O'C is better.

Letter to Leo J. Zuber, Spring 1961

Cogitating the Critic *piece. Could you maybe get me "The Resurrection" by FX Durrell, S&W?*

Cross Currents

Edited by Joseph E. Cunneen. West Nyack, N.Y., Quarterly.

The Bulletin, April 1, 1961

Of the many magazines in America published through the initiative of Catholics, the one which makes the most important contribution to Catholic intellectual life in this country is unfortunately the one least known to a wide audience. This is *Cross Currents*, a quarterly review which reprints articles from all over the world on theology, philosophy, the arts and social thought. These articles are the best that can be found on religious subjects as they impinge on the modern world, or on modern discoveries as they impinge on the Judeo-Christian tradition. The articles serve to fertilize Catholic life with currents of thought from other religions and from those of our own which the average communicant is not apt to come by. The magazine serves an ecumenical purpose since it acquaints Catholics with critiques of famous Protestant and Jewish theologians and acquaints its many Protestant readers with the best in Catholic thought. Barth, Tillich, Cullman and Buber are frequently represented in its pages as well as such Catholic thinkers as Guardini, Marcel, and the late Fr. Teilhard.

The magazine was founded in 1950 by a group of Catholic laymen, its aim to "explore the implications of Christianity for our times." None of its articles is abridged or popularized, no one article is exhausted by a first or second reading, but all are accessible to any reasonably active mind. The editors would like to see *Cross Currents* used as a basis for discussions in small parish groups. Since the use of the mind is seldom encouraged in parish activities, this seems unlikely of fulfillment, but for any individual concerned to discover the deep currents of Christian thought, this magazine is invaluable.

The Conversion of Augustine

Romano Guardini. Newman, 1960.

The Bulletin, May 27, 1961

In his introduction to this analysis of St. Augustine's odyssey, Msgr. Guardini notes two approaches usual in dealing with his subject, both of which he has tried to avoid. One of these sees the Confessions as a record of a conversion from evil to good, the outcome only being of interest, the hesitations along the way of no real significance. This view leaves out of account the living man, ignores his psychology and ends with merely theoretical insights. The other approach goes to the opposite extreme and makes psychology and the living process everything and ends seeing the subject as a case history. Msgr. Guardini has steered well in between these two approaches and has produced a psychological study well informed on spiritual realities. He unfolds Augustine's story on ethical levels and on the levels of mind and idea as well. The result is as penetrating a study of the saint as we are liable to get.

The book is divided into two parts, the first of which is designed to elucidate some of the key Augustinian ideas. It seems unfortunate that this more abstract material had to be put by itself at the beginning. The second part, which is an interpretation of Augustine's spiritual drama, is the more readable section. In any case, it is good to have a book on St. Augustine by Msgr. Guardini.

The Critic: A Catholic Review of Books and the Arts

Thomas More Association.

The Bulletin, June 10, 1961

Since its beginning, the magazine of the Thomas More Association has gone through a series of changes which, it is to be hoped, parallel the American Catholic's attitude toward books and the arts. The magazine began in 1942 as *Books on Trial*, a name which reflected the Catholic preoccupation for grading and judging books in accordance with their likelihood of dealing blows to the reader's Faith. *Books on Trial* offered eleven possible verdicts on the books reviewed; the legal atmosphere was thick. The magazine eventually dropped the verdicts and then dropped the name. It is now called *The Critic: A Catholic Review of Books and the Arts.* There is in the designation, Catholic Review of Books and the Arts, the implied assumption that there is a brand of criticism special to Catholics rather than that any good criticism will reflect a Catholic view of reality. The ghost of *Books on Trial* is hard to lay.

The Critic has in each issue three or four articles on cultural subjects and about fifty short reviews of current books, fiction and non-fiction. The articles on music and the arts are usually better than the articles on literature, which too frequently are about minor Catholic liturgy [literary] figures, or when about non-Catholic writers tend to show that these are Catholic in spite of themselves and therefore acceptable. The reviews of books on social thought, history and religion are better than the fiction reviews. Fiction is considered by most Catholic readers to be a waste of time, and *The Critic,* which recently began publishing a story or two an issue, has taken a step which may prove dangerous to its circulation. Already letters have appeared in the letters column expressing displeasure that this space should be, in effect, wasted. This may well be true since one feels that the fiction which the majority of Catholics will put up with will be, while not commercial fiction, still an innocuous variety that could as well be done without. *The Critic* also occasionally devotes space to poetry and recently published a large selection of the verse of living American Catholic poets. The poetry will probably be tolerated, though not read, and the fiction read but not tolerated.

The metamorphosis of *The Critic,* however, is not yet complete. Beginning in the fall the magazine will publish nine or ten articles in each issue, there will be fewer but longer and more thorough reviews, and the subtitle will be changed from "A Catholic Review of Books and the Arts" to "A Magazine of Christian Culture." All these changes promise a better magazine, one which will be less parochial and which will lead as well as reflect the American Catholic's growing appetite for the arts.

The Critic is well worth the price of a subscription.

Stop Pushing

Dan Herr. Hanover House, 1961.

The Bulletin, June 10, 1961

Mr. Dan Herr's chief talent is for the pursuit and exposure of idiotic printed matter. He is at his best when bringing to public attention the advertising in the Catholic press (although this entails no more than copying it out word for word) or when he sets up a mirror before the lady's magazines, the horror of which is that it is in no measure a distorting mirror. When he confines himself to such public services, Mr. Herr is at least endurable, sometimes enjoyable, and always valuable.

Columnists in general, however, and those with pretensions to humor in particular, would be well advised to let the impact of their talents come to the public in well-regulated dribbles, to scatter rather than to collect their pieces. Embedded in the general earnestness of *The Critic*, these columns manage to thrust themselves forward with a certain vitriolic verve, which when collected, by some obscure law of accumulation, becomes bluster. The humorist cannot allow himself to see two sides of any question unless he is a very complicated humorist. Mr. Herr does not sport an ounce of complication and he depends for his effects 95%

of the time on exaggeration alone. While his opinions are in general sound—witness his disaffection for the teen-ager—there is a sameness about their presentation that makes it advisable to let a long period of time elapse between reading one piece and the next; anytime from two months to a year.

Letter to Leo J. Zuber, June 24, 1961

I am speeding Leclerc back to you. That is not my dish of tea. I am always open to Old Testament Studies. If you happen to get "The Old Testament and Modern Studies," H. H. Rowley, Oxford, I'll take it. I still owe you the Guardini which I am trying to finish. I'll take that "Bible & the Ancient Near East" 61–157 on your list.

Life's Long Journey

Kenneth Walker. Nelson, 1961.

The Bulletin, June 24, 1961

This is a book on evolution written for the general reader. Its author, a medical doctor, believes that the scientist who is a non-specialist has, because of his overall view, a great deal to contribute to this subject. He traces the evolution of the human species up to the present where he sees man facing a crisis. Dr. Walker's contention is that man's future evolution will be along spiritual lines. Teilhard is never mentioned in this book, which is a peculiar oversight since he is one of the few modern evolutionists who believes in spiritual evolution and a much greater exponent of it than Dr. Walker.

This may be explained by the author's obvious distaste for the Church's stand on birth control which Dr. Walker believes should be one of the chief factors in our effort to direct evolution. No attempt is made to do justice to or even to understand the Catholic position on this subject. It is dismissed as superstition and the fatuous observation is made that the Church sanctions death control but not birth control. Dr. Walker apparently sees this as a grave inconsistency.

There is much of value in this book. As long as the doctor sticks to his science, he has something to offer. When he becomes a philosopher and social planner he oversteps his limits.

The Meaning of Grace

Charles Journet. Kenedy, 1960.

The Bulletin, July 22, 1961

This is a short work on the subject of grace by one of the Church's leading theologians. Abbé Journet pays particular attention to the disagreement between Catholic and Protestant theologians on the subject of grace and predestination, Divine foreknowledge and the initiating of evil acts. He describes the grace of Adam, the grace by anticipation under the Mosaic law, the grace which we enjoy now in what he calls the Age of the Holy Ghost, when graces are received through the sacraments, and lastly the uncovenanted graces which are given to those peoples who do not know Christ as the Church knows Him. This work is lucid and simple and brings the subject within the grasp of those without theological training.

Selected Letters of Stephen Vincent Benét

Edited by Charles Fenton. Yale University Press, 1960.

The Bulletin, August 5, 1961

The epithet "best-loved poet" usually speaks more for the man than his poetry, and after his death it will lead more often to a collection of his letters than to a critical appraisal of his work. Stephen Vincent Benét was known for his gay spirit and warm friendships and a quality of both is apparent in his letters. They also say a good deal about the literary life in the twenties and thirties among Benét's circle and they say even more about the taste of the fiction-reading public, then as now. Benét struggled to make a living by free-lance writing for the popular magazines. In 1926, he wrote to his wife, "I wrote another story yesterday and am typing it today. It is called 'Bon Voyage' and is a dear little candy-laxative of a tale about a sweet little girl named Sally. I do not see how it can fail to sell—it is so cheap." Whether Benét could have written better poetry had he not had this burden constantly upon him, the letters cannot tell us, but they make sad reading since they suggest the possibility.

Letter to Leo J. Zuber, August 22, 1961

I am sending you back The Briar Patch . . . *and* The Son of Man. *I have already reviewed* The Son of Man *for the* Bulletin*!!! Some time ago. I've got the first review copy on my shelves. The other two I'll keep. I now owe you 4 reviews.*

When will we see you all & little Zubers?

The Resurrection

F. X. Durrwell, C.Ss.R. Sheed & Ward, 1960.

The Bulletin, September 16, 1961

This detailed and excellent theological study seeks to restore the resurrection to its proper place in the theology of the redemption, which has been truncated by thought which pays exclusive attention to Christ's death. This situation came about in those centuries when the redemption was seen solely as a satisfaction for sin.

With the rise of Biblical scholarship, the resurrection is again taking its place as central to the redemption. Père Durrwell's study, which was first published in France in 1950, has become the standard work on the subject. It presents a synthesis of all the Bible says about the resurrection as part of the mystery of salvation and considers the life of the Church in the risen Christ. In a note to the second edition Père Durrwell draws the reader's attention to two vital truths which emerge from a study of the resurrection: "the fact that the death and resurrection remain forever actual in Christ in glory, and the identification of the Church with Christ in glory, not merely in one body with him, but actually in the act of his death and glorification."

The liturgical revival has sought to give Catholics a new consciousness of the full splendor of the message of salvation and this requires a rediscovery of the resurrection. According to Charles Davis, who supplies an introduction to Père Durrwell's study, this is the reason few books in recent times are more important than this one.

Themes of the Bible

J. Guillet, S.J. Fides, 1961.

The Bulletin, September 16, 1961

Themes of the Bible is essentially a study of religious language and its supernatural character. It is not intended to be an exhaustive study but is meant to open up new perspectives of meaning through the study of the words in sacred scripture. A selection of Biblical themes—the exodus, grace, justice, sin, damnation—are used to highlight the progress of Revelation and to show that the religious language of Israel is the work of the Spirit of God as well as its human authors. Père Guillet's thesis is that "in its most diverse forms, whether in the great work of a Moses, in the vibrant heart of a poet, in the wise man's daily effort at being faithful to the Law, in the message of the prophets, God was blazing his paths." The histories of certain key words are traced through the Old Testament where their supernatural character remains obscure into the New where it is manifested fully when Christ appears. Here "Revelation bursts forth in a definitive manner."

The general reader will find this study illuminating as well as the student of Biblical criticism.

Letter to Leo J. Zuber, September 23, 1961

I'll do Jubilee *but I never see* The Ga. Review. *If you take it and want to send me some representative samples of it, I'll see what I can do.*

Thanks for the two new books.

The Mediaeval Mystics of England

Eric Colledge. Scribners, 1961.

The Bulletin, September 30, 1961

This anthology contains selected writings from seven of the best known mystics of mediaeval England: St. Aelred of Rievaulx, St. Edmund Rich, Richard Rolle, Walter Hilton, Julian of Norwich, and the unknown author of the "Cloud of Unknowing." The latter is represented here by the less well-known "Book of Privy Counsel," which, of these selections, seems to the reviewer by far the most interesting. Both Hilton and the author of "The Book of Privy Counsel" were concerned to dispel the indiscreet and enthusiastic ideas about mysticism that had come about through the popularity of earlier writers such as Richard Rolle. To cut across futile intellectualizing in prayer, the author of "The Book of Privy Counsel" advises his monks to come down to the lowest level of their intelligence and think "not what you are, but that you are."

Eric Colledge, a lecturer in English literature at Liverpool University, has supplied a scholarly introduction which the newcomer to these writers will find beyond him but which will be of value to students of the period and of mysticism.

Letter to Leo J. Zuber, October 7, 1961

Two books down and two to go. I wrote Oona Sullivan at Jubilee *to send me some information about themselves. Meantime I will make the acquaintance of the* GA Review.

Freedom, Grace, and Destiny

Romano Guardini. Pantheon, 1961.

The Bulletin, October 28, 1961

Msgr. Guardini here explores the Christian understanding of freedom, grace and destiny, three interrelated concepts which in modern thought have been distorted, discarded, or diluted in a fashion that suggests Satanic influence. Msgr. Guardini treats each concept in a separate chapter, asking first how it is presented in immediate experience, what revelation has to say about it, and finally what is its significance for the whole pattern of existence. In all his work Msgr. Guardini's directive is this attempt to view the pattern of Christian existence as a whole, as it was viewed in early and medieval Christian thought before philosophy became separated from theology, empirical science from philosophy, and practical instruction from knowledge of reality. He is concerned that this conscious unity of existence has been lost to a large extent even by believing Christians. "The believer no longer stands with his faith amid the concrete, actual world, and he no longer rediscovers that world by his faith. He has made a grim necessity of this dismemberment by constructing, if we may employ the term, a chemically pure faith in which he insists upon seeing the true form of orthodoxy. This orthodoxy has a somewhat austere and very courageous quality, but we must not forget that it is an emergency position." This is an important book. Msgr. Guardini has admirably carried out his intentions.

Letter to Leo J. Zuber, November 19, 1961

This clears me up on the reviews. I'll take #61–311 off your list if you've still got it. What about Philip Hughes' new book on the Councils? Hope you do the Mary Ann yourself.

Letter to Leo J. Zuber, undated

Two down and one to go. Could you get me "The Church in Crisis" Philip Hughes, Hanover House, $4.95.

If you want to see two Andalusia peachickens in the heart of Atlanta, go visit the Cancer Home. They came for them yesterday.

The Range of Reason

Jacques Maritain. Scribners, 1961.

The Bulletin, November 25, 1961

In this book made up of ten chapters from *Raison et Raisons* and eight essays from other sources, Maritain covers a variety of philosophical topics and their social extensions, in which the range of reason can be illustrated. The age of the Enlightenment substituted reason for revelation, with the result that confidence in reason has gradually decayed until in the present age, which doubts also fact and value, reason finds few supporters outside of Neo-Thomist philosophy. Maritain's has been one of the major voices in modern philosophy to reassert the primacy of reason. All his work springs from confidence in it. He puts it in the proper perspective, where it serves and not substitutes for revelation.

This book contains abridged discussions of most of the subjects that Maritain has devoted whole works to. Most readers who have any interest in Maritain at all will prefer the longer works on these various topics, but *The Range of Reason* is good for introducing those new to Maritain to the wide range of his thought.

Letter to Leo J. Zuber, November 28, 1961

I sure did like the review of the Mary Ann book. Maybe you all will be at that book party the SCLA are giving on the 10th. If so I'll hope to see you as I am supposed to be present, as salesman I presume.*

Send me any scourgy book you like for my advent penance.

*Apparently this refers to the Catholic Laymen's Association, the organization responsible for the publication of *The Bulletin.*

The Bible and the Ancient Near East

Edited by G. E. Wright. Doubleday, 1961.

The Old Testament and Modern Study

Edited by H. H. Rowley. Oxford Paperbacks, 1961.

The Bulletin, December 9, 1961

These two books are collections of essays written by Ancient Near East scholars for other Ancient Near East scholars. *The Bible and the Ancient Near East* is a memorial volume in honor of William Foxwell Albright, one of the country's foremost Oriental scholars, who retired as Professor of Semitic Languages and Chairman of the Oriental Seminary at Johns Hopkins University in 1958. *The Old Testament and Modern Study* is a volume issued by the Society for Old Testament Study. Its aim is to survey the significant work that has been done in the field in the last thirty years in order to bring out the new trends that have appeared.

Although these essays are for the professional scholar, they offer the lay public some fascinating insights into what is involved in discovering ancient civilizations and languages. Ironically, as more material, through excavation and more accurate methods of dating, becomes available, interpretation grows increasingly difficult. Nineteenth century Biblical scholarship, which wrecked the faith of so many, has been almost entirely discredited and the historical value of many Biblical texts attested to by chronologies worked out by radio-carbon dating and the comparison of cultures. There is a healthy sense in these books that as our knowledge of the past grows, the mystery of it grows likewise.

Teilhard de Chardin

Oliver Rabut, O.P. Sheed & Ward, 1961.

The Bulletin, December 23, 1961

This is the best critical evaluation of the work of Père Teilhard de Chardin to appear in this country. Most of the studies written on Teilhard's thought have been either uncritically enthusiastic or uncritically condemnatory. Oliver Rabut understands Teilhard's greatness without accepting as proven or even likely many of his hypotheses. He believes that Teilhard yields to a temptation to overemphasize the element of psychism in nature and that he does not distinguish adequately between the supernatural action of Christ and the purely natural ascent of evolution. He also feels that one of Teilhard's mistakes lay in not realizing that, past a certain point, it was necessary for him to change his discipline from science to philosophy and then to theology.

On the positive side he believes that those who condemn Teilhard never see what it is in him that makes him so attractive nor "the means of justifying one's final capitulation to him." He was a scientist who saw deeply certain intellectual and spiritual needs of our times. "The solutions he proposes, imperfect though they may be, are already such as can be used; at times they are excellent." The discovery that we owe to Teilhard is that vocation of spirit is visible, concrete, and of absorbing interest. If his method did not achieve all he thought it did, he was still making an attempt which it is necessary for scientists and theologians to take over and carry further.

This is a brilliant book which will be of great value to any one interested in Teilhard.

The Novelist and the Passion Story

F. W. Dillistone. Sheed & Ward, 1960.

The Bulletin, December 23, 1961

This is a study of an Episcopal theologian of four novels consciously intended by their authors to suggest the passion of Christ and its redemptive power. The novels are Mauriac's *The Lamb*, Melville's *Billy Budd*, Kazantzakis' *The Great Passion*, and Faulkner's *A Fable*, representing respectively,

Catholic, Calvinist, Greek and roughly Lutheran theology.

It is interesting to note as an indication of the difficulty of attempting the Christ figure that Mauriac and Faulkner are represented by what most critics agree are their worst books. *Billy Budd* is considered a classic but there is some doubt whether Melville actually intended its hero to be a Christ figure, though Dean Dillistone makes a good case for it. He goes through each novel thoroughly, tracing the pattern of the passion and its redemptive effects and then in a final chapter, discusses what Auden calls "the insolubility of the religious paradox in aesthetic terms," and indicates the point of failure in each book. He suggests that Mauriac's weakness is to resolve the paradox by some miraculous event. He considers this the weakness of Catholic theology generally. To the reviewer it appears a strictly novelistic weakness. In any case Dean Dillistone can accommodate a good deal of heresy in his Christ figures.

The book is an interesting study of attempts which by their nature must fail.

Joseph, Son of David

Sister Emily Joseph, C.S.J. St. Anthony's Guild Press, 1961.

Unpublished Review

This pamphlet contains a meditation on St. Joseph for each week in the year, each meditation written by a different person, and they are as different as Cardinal Vaughan and Dorothy Day. Material from the apocryphal writings has been avoided and some attempt has been made to consider diversity of approach and literary excellence. Not much diversity of approach is possible however, and not a great deal of literary excellence is to be found on this subject.

Reason and Revelation in the Middle Ages

Étienne Gilson. Scribners, 1961.

Unpublished Review

These are three lectures delivered by Gilson at the University of Virginia in 1937 on the relation between theology and philosophy in the Middle Ages. Briefly he traces three spiritual families which dominated thought at one time or another during the seven centuries that make up the period, taking first what he calls "the family of Tertullian," which gave the primacy to faith, and showing how the early conflict between faith and reason was synthesized by St. Augustine. He then discusses the origin of modern rationalism, which entered the thought of the Middle Ages with Averroës, and the synthesis of its conflict with faith, effected by St. Thomas. He indicates that the disastrous rise of nominalism came about when the Thomistic synthesis was ignored.

These lectures are an excellent introduction to Gilson's *The Unity of Philosophical Experience*, a book indispensable to an understanding of the modern age. In addition to the intellectual value of anything written by Gilson, it is always a pleasure to read him for the vigor and lucidity of his style.

The Phenomenon of Man

Pierre Teilhard de Chardin. Harper, 1959.

The American Scholar, Fall 1961

The Phenomenon of Man by P. Teilhard de Chardin is a work that demands the attention of scientist, theologian and poet.

It is a search for human significance in the evolutionary process. Because Teilhard is both a man of science and a believer, the scientist and the theologian will require considerable time to sift and evaluate his thought, but the poet, whose sight is essentially prophetic, will at once recognize in Teilhard a kindred intelligence. His is a scientific expression of what the poet attempts to do: penetrate matter until spirit is revealed in it. Teilhard's vision sweeps forward without detaching itself at any point from the earth.

Editor's note: This is the only one of Flannery O'Connor's reviews to appear in a secular publication. Reprinted from *The American Scholar* 30, no. 4 (Fall 1961).

reviews and letters

1962

Conversations with Cassandra

Sr. M. Madeleva. Macmillan, 1961.

The Bulletin, January 6, 1962

This book consists largely of short talks which Sister Madeleva has given to the students at St. Mary's College at Notre Dame where she has been president for 27 years. She discusses Christian education for women, its goals, its purpose, and the kind of woman she hopes will be its end result.

There are two chapters included which apparently were not talks to students. One is called "Conversations with Children." In it Sister Madeleva recounts several conversations she has had with young children who make various wise comments on life, art, and the world in general. These children are very hard to take. The other is about Dame Julian of Norwich and is one of the best chapters in the book.

For the reader not specifically interested in Catholic education this book will seem repetitious and a trifle dull, dull not by virtue of its intellectual content which is splendid, but by a rather high-blown style which soon exhausts the reader. For those parents who are debating whether to send their daughter to a Catholic college, the book is a good one. They will probably be convinced that she will get something there that she wouldn't get elsewhere.

Talk Sense!

Edward Gryst, S.J. Macmillan, 1961.

The Bulletin, February 3, 1962

Here is a book suitable for teaching philosophy to school boys, and it is written in the form of conversations between a philosophy professor and a hat salesman. The conversations, meant to be funny, for a time are. According to the jacket, "if there is any such thing as 'painless profundity' this book is it—unless, of course, you split your sides laughing." You are not liable to do that and how much effortless philosophy you will learn from this book is also doubtful. There is, interwoven in these conversations, a complete system of philosophical reasoning with all its principles and complexities, and at the end of each short chapter a summary statement of the principles discussed. The sugar coating dissolves quickly and the philosophy is left intact, as difficult as always to digest. School boys, however, will probably like this book and might even acquire from it a taste for the use of reason.

Letter to Leo J. Zuber, February 13, 1962

I am sending you back this book of essays so you can send it to Mr. Koab. Just as well to have somebody else do some of the Teilhard. Harper is going to bring out a book of his letters ("Letters from a Traveller") on July 4 and you could get that for Mr. K. They have already sent me bound galleys and I think it's great. If you know anybody who would just love this yer "Conscience and Its Right to Freedom," I will be glad to part with it too.

I'm sort of interested in Karl Rahner, S.J. if you get in anything of his.

Your flu story beats mine but I'm glad I've had it now as I have three lectures to give in April and May and would not like to pull your stunt then.

Tell the liberry people they ought to read something besides "Catholic" books. They don't know how the other half lives.

When *are we going to get a Bishop? High time they got us something.*

Letter to Leo J. Zuber, February 17, 1962

Think I can do without the Maisie Ward—Houselander one. I'm stuck on "Conscience & Its Right to Freedom."

What about Roland de Vaux's Ancient Israel*?*

Christian Faith and Man's Religion

Marc C. Ebersole. Crowell, 1961.

Christianity Divided

Edited by Callahan, Oberman, and O'Hanlon. Sheed & Ward, 1961.

The Bulletin, February 17, 1962

Christian Faith and Man's Religion, a study of five non-Catholic religious thinkers, is based on the distinction between religion simply as man's deep involvement with his own existence, not necessarily from a theistic point of view, and the specific belief in Christ as the God who has redeemed us. Much of the thought of these men, with the exception of Barth and Fromm, is an effort to fit Christianity into a frame of the 18th century enlightenment. Fromm rejects Christianity entirely in favor of natural religion; Barth rejects religion entirely and sees the Christian faith as a judgment against it. Bonhoeffer rejects religion on the grounds that man has outgrown it but accepts the Christian faith; Schleiermacher sees the Christian faith as the fulfillment of religion but makes this faith dependent on feeling. Niebuhr emerges as the most balanced and most nearly orthodox of the five. He sees the Christian faith as both the judgment against and the fulfillment of religion.

Aside from several references to St. Augustine and one to St. Thomas, it is nowhere suggested that any thought took place before the time of Luther. This is a fascinating book for any Catholic who wants to understand better the problems and achievements of Protestant theology.

An equally fascinating and more profound book is *Christianity Divided*, a collection of theological essays by Protestant and Catholic scholars on the fundamental issues which divide them—scripture and tradition, hermeneutics, the Church, the sacraments, and justification. The aim of the book is to make available to a wider audience some of the significant works of important theologians in critical areas of ecumenical discussion. The selections will reveal new directions in Protestant and Catholic thought that are not as well known as they deserve to be.

Jubilee

Edited by Edward Rice. A.M.D.G. Publishing Co.

The Bulletin, February 17, 1962

Jubilee is a partly pictorial monthly magazine which should be of interest to those who would like to see more taste and imagination in popular Catholic journalism than is usually found there. After some years of planning and search for the necessary funds, Edward Rice published the first issue of *Jubilee* in 1953. Since Mr. Rice's plan included insistence on good taste in advertising, funds were hard to come by, but *Jubilee* has continued to appear despite difficulties of this kind and now has a circulation of 50,000.

A magazine "of the Church and her people," as *Jubilee* calls itself, could easily become a grab-bag of pictures and stories of merely topical interest, but *Jubilee* is guided by a controlling intelligence with a strong historical sense and the intention of making manifest the universality of the Church. The emphasis is on ecumenism, particularly with the Eastern churches, the liturgy, social issues, and Catholic culture around the world. These stories are always well written and illustrated with excellent photographs. The art work in *Jubilee* makes subject for vigorous debate in its letters column. The editors have a predilection for printing their stories on colored paper of various bilious or harrowing shades of green, blue and yellow. One can expect to find a double page devoted wholly to a two-line liturgical fish or a red ball. The reader can tolerate this since it is a healthy reaction to so much bad religious art of a different and worse kind. A subscription to *Jubilee* extends one's knowledge of the Church and one's pleasure in it. It is a magazine to be recommended highly.

Editor's note: This review was illustrated with a rough, irregular, childlike drawing of a red ball.

Letter to Leo J. Zuber, George Washington's Birthday, 1962

Well we got us a bishop but beyond that who knows what?

I will, I will send back Conscience and Its Right to Freedom. *I don't care about Paul Smith. On this list I'd like the Hilda Graef volume. I've read part of* The Cardinal Spellman Story *in* Look. *It is really a shocking sort of book. Very bad for the public image of the Church. If you want me to review it, I will.*

The Georgia Review

University of Georgia, Quarterly.

The Bulletin, March 2, 1962

The word which might best characterize *The Georgia Review* is "pleasant." It is, apparently by design, one of the least intellectually strenuous of the college quarterlies. Critics do not criticize the criticism of other critic's critics in the pages of *The Georgia Review.* There are no battles in the footnotes; in fact, no footnotes. It is obviously a magazine by Southerners for Southerners about Southerners. Its manner is so relaxed as to suggest genial front-porch monologues* by local scholars whom it is not necessary to listen to very attentively. Though occasionally an article about a living Southern writer or politician, or about some non-Southerner, such as Robert Frost, may make its way into these pages, most of the articles are about little known or forgotten Georgia literary or historical figures—Frances Newman, William Harris Crawford. These articles are invariably well-written. *The Georgia Review* also prints poems and stories. Its poems are well-turned and undemanding. Its fiction, with only an occasional exception, leaves the impression that it has travelled much and been rejected many times before finding asylum here. It is the magazine's worst feature. All in all, *The Georgia Review* is an unpretentious, and by that much, refreshing quarterly, admirably suited to the Georgia temper.

*Published as "monolgoies."

Evidence of Satan in the Modern World

Leon Christiani. Macmillan, 1961.

The Bulletin, March 2, 1962

It is ironical that in these evil times we should need fresh evidence of the existence of Satan, but such is the case. According to Baudelaire, the devil's greatest wile is to persuade us he does not exist. The Christian drama is meaningless without Satan, but only recently there has been considerable publicity about a dispute among Anglicans over whether the devil should be allowed to remain in their catechism. Such is the trend of the times.

In *Evidence of Satan in the Modern World*, Leon Christiani traces demonic activity from New Testament times to the 20th century, concentrating heavily on cases of possession. Although the modern reader will find his credulity strained by some of the macabre instances of possession described, he will be required by a strictly scientific attitude not to dismiss this evidence out of hand. The jacket tells us that this book is well documented and presented in an unsensational manner. The documentation here has to be accepted on the word of the author and the subject is sensational *per se.*

The author's discussions of the more generalized activities of Satan are less disturbing to the credulity although their implications are a good deal more terrifying. All in all, the reader leaves this book with his belief in Satan considerably fortified.

Letter to Leo J. Zuber, March 9, 1962

I'll relieve you of No. 5—Old Niebuhr, or if nobody else wants it the Küng or Lynch. The Kinderbeast Prize *sounds suspiciously like poetry. Don't know the good sister.*

Oona Sullivan wrote and thanked me for doing the piece on Jubilee *and said she thought the illustration of the "baby whale asleep brightened the page considerably."*

In the Ga. Review *one* its *got written* it's. *This was undoubtedly my fault. When you read mine over please check for that kind of carelessness, to which I am liable.*

I thought you might want to put in a notice about this new Mentor-Omega series from NAL.

Letter to Leo J. Zuber, undated

Thanks for the clippings. I'm a doctor of letters, non-negotiable. I can wear the hood to feed the peafowl.*

I seem to be going in for biographies of cardinals.

*An honorary Doctor of Letters degree from St. Mary's College at Notre Dame.

The Conscience of Israel

Bruce Vawter, C.M. Sheed & Ward, 1961.

The Bulletin, March 17, 1962

In *The Conscience of Israel*, Fr. Vawter analyzes the pre-exilic prophets of the eighth and seventh centuries B.C., Amos, Hosea, Micah, Isaiah and Jeremiah and the minor prophets, Nahum, Sephaniah and Habakkuk, and attempts to reset their words in the concrete historical moment that brought them forth. Nineteenth century Biblical criticism was largely that of liberal Protestantism. The result of this was that the prophets were seen in the light of liberal Protestant concerns. They became Israelite Luthers and Wesleys, innovators opposing ritualism, or social reformers of advanced views. Twentieth century Biblical criticism has returned the prophets to their genuine mission, which was not to innovate, but to recall the people to truths they were already well aware of but chose to ignore. Victorian commentators appear sometimes to have thought of the prophets as "liberal vicars or non-conformist chaplains . . . with the same bluff piety that made the Empire great." Fr. Vawter restores them to their exotic Oriental culture where they were seen by their contemporaries as inspired men, in communication with "that otherness that men have always associated with the divine." In this setting alone it is possible to understand an Isaiah walking naked as a warning to Egypt, and Hosea agonizing over his prostitute wife or an Ezekiel baking his bread over dung to symbolize the destruction to come.

Fr. Vawter warns against making Christians of the prophets. The prophets prepared for the revelation of the New Testament; they did not anticipate it. This excellent book will give the reader a fuller understanding of both preparation and fulfillment.

Letter to Leo J. Zuber, March 26, 1962

This [Mailer] is beyond me. . . . I don't know who you are going to be able to unload this on.

Thanks for the others. It's going to take me some time.

The Victorian Vision

Margaret M. Maison. Sheed & Ward, 1961.

The Bulletin, March 31, 1962

The favorite subject of the Victorians was religion. From Tractarian to Dissenter to Latitudinarian, their pre-occupation was with questions of man's right relationship to God. Even Agnosticism as it began to take over toward the end of the period took on the lineaments of a religion. Dr. Maison in *The Victorian Vision* analyzes Victorian religious opinion as it is seen in popular novels of the period. Most of the novels she discusses are unashamedly propagandistic, badly written, and to the modern reader sources of high comedy. One of the funniest aspects of these novels was the treatment of the villain of the Protestant imagination—the Jesuit. He was "a spy, a secret agent, suave, supercilious and satanically unscrupulous, laying his cunning plots for the submission of England to 'Jesuitocracy,' wheedling rich widows, forcing his converts to change their wills in favor of his order, to kneel in penitence for hours through chilly nights and to leave their families at a minute's notice."

Not all the religious novelists of the period were of this stamp. Both Newman and Manning wrote novels as well as Disraeli. Dr. Maison has read an incredible number of these books, both good and bad, and analyzes them with zest. The result is one of the most enjoyable and enlightening books that have been written about the Victorian temper.

Letter to Leo J. Zuber, May 7, 1962

Thanks for sending this but I am so far behind on my reviews that I had better not take any more until I do what I have. I have been traveling around giving lectures. Just got back yesterday from Chicago and Notre Dame. I had lunch with Paul Cuneo and Joel Wells and Joel Wells drove me over to Notre Dame. They both inquired after you.

I recently lectured at Converse where I ran into Bill Davidson who edits the Ga. Review. *He upbraided me on "damning with faint praise" his sainted organ.*

Letter to Leo J. Zuber, undated

If you come by "Prince of Democracy: James Cardinal Gibbons" by Boucher & Tehan, Hanover House, $4.95, I'd be cheered to review it.

Toward the Knowledge of God

Claude Tresmontant. Helicon, 1961.

The Bulletin, May 12, 1962

In this essay Père Tresmontant demonstrates three ways of showing the possibility of knowing that God exists. The problem is first approached from the standpoint of human thought attaining to the knowledge of the Absolute when it has as its point of departure a consideration of reality. In this section the phenomenon of Israel is not brought in. In the second section the problem is approached by discussing Israel. Tresmontant shows that such a local and particular phenomenon may nevertheless contain a lesson of universal import. In this approach any consideration of Christ is omitted. In the last section the person of Jesus is considered for what He may teach about the Absolute.

Tresmontant is convinced that a knowledge of God is really possible by a correct use of human reason, beginning with the fact of creation and without asking the unbeliever to make Kierkegaard's leap into the absurd. He does not suggest that this quest for God could have reached its destination without the guidance of Judaism and Christianity or if there had been no manifestation of the Absolute to man, but this "only proves that the human mind is congenitally affected by a weakness or difficulty in conceiving of reality, life, the spiritual or the new."

This closely reasoned book will reward a careful reading.

Letter to Leo J. Zuber, July 8, 1962

Two down & one to go. I'll take the Teilhard if nobody else will. There's just been a warning about him from the Holy Office but he was not put on the Index. I will take due account in the reviews; though on second thought it might be better to send the book to a clerical gentleman if you have any on your list.

Letter to Leo J. Zuber, July 30, 1962

Thanks for greetings from the Nation's Capitol. I've never been there. I doubt if I can even spell it.

These records you asked about—are they music? I'm not asking for myself—a friend of mine who is head of the Dept. of Communications Arts at Notre Dame used to review records for Ave Maria. *They got a new man because they wanted something not so high brow. The last time I saw him he was looking around for somewhere to review records for. He's in Europe right now, but if you are interested I can send you his home address & you can write him in Sept. If they knew you had a good record man, they might be quicker about sending records.*

Enclose review. Many more to go. Has anybody asked for "The Photo Album of St. Therese of Lisieux"—Kenedy? Be glad to have it myself.

Letter to Leo J. Zuber, August 3, 1962

It's getting dangerous to write reviews for the Bulletin*! In the review of the Hans Küng book* "engender" has been made into "endanger." I can't find my carbon but I don't think this was my error. Correction: I have just found my carbon & it isn't my error. I think this ought to be corrected since it is such a fine book.*

In the other review they have me calling something "a opportunistic individual" when I am sure I wrote "an." This isn't important as I don't mind trifles but I think making engender endanger *ought to be corrected.*

Who ever tampers with these things is [a] great tamperer. I once wrote "gnostic" and they made it "agnostic."

*The review appeared in *The Bulletin,* August 4, 1962. She was apparently responding immediately upon receipt of her copy.

The Council, Reform and Reunion

Hans Küng. Sheed & Ward, 1961.

The Integrating Mind

William F. Lynch, S.J. Sheed & Ward, 1962.

The Bulletin, August 4, 1962

If the Church were equipped with a reverse Index which required that certain books be read, these two would deserve a high place on the list. The wide distribution of *The Council, Reform and Reunion* at this time would engender* a realistic attitude toward the coming council and would perhaps stimulate the laity to participate in it through prayer. It would seem that an event of this magnitude in the Church's life would inspire more enthusiasm among Catholics, but the majority, being uninformed, take it lightly. Fr. Küng first sets forth the need of constant renewal in the Church, which, because she has the limitation of taking her earthly shape from the age, is subject to constant deformation. In the present age, it is indispensable that we make a "painfully criticial dispassionate analysis, the kind of description which will appear one-sided, of the weaknesses in the Church's position." Fr. Küng proceeds relentlessly to do this. He is careful to point out the difference between the kind of restoration which took place during the last period of the Council of Trent and a genuine reform which would imply creative growth through a real understanding of the Protestant Reformer's demands. Particularly interesting is his discussion of the Petrine office and its relation to episcopal initiative, but on every point this book has something to offer. No Catholic can read it without profit to himself and the Church.

The Integrating Mind re-emphasizes and reinforces themes

found in Fr. Lynch's two previous books, *The Image Industries* and *Christ and Apollo*. It is an essay against the totalistic temptation—in history, politics and art—which rigidly separates categories into either/or choices. Fr. Lynch makes clear that he is writing here of contraries, not contradictions. The book, "in substance a plea that we keep things together that belong together," is timely, though not topical, and should serve as an antidote to prevailing exaggerations in American political and social thought.

*Published "endanger"; see preceding letter.

The Cardinal Spellman Story

Robert I. Gannon, S.J. Doubleday, 1962.

The Bulletin, August 4, 1962

To the Protestant Cardinal Spellman is the image of the Church in America. It was therefore with consternation that many Catholics read the condensed version of Fr. Gannon's biography of the Cardinal in *Look*. The image created there was of an opportunistic individual, innocently aggressive, who fitted well into a church where prelates were more concerned with protocol than piety. Fortunately the book itself mitigates this image, and leaves one wondering who produced the condensation and with what malice aforethought.

Cardinal Spellman moves through *The Cardinal Spellman Story* round, smiling, efficient and indefatigable. Largely through a few letters written home from servicemen, which seem absolutely trustworthy, the reader gets a picture of a very humble and simple man, one gladly willing to say Mass in the rain in Korea on Christmas day when he could more easily have been elsewhere. Such glimpses are stuck here and there in a mass of official material, some of it fascinating, a good deal of it tedious. We are given many official letters and telegrams verbatim and sizable portions of the Cardinal's sermons. Cardinal Spellman has apparently often given as many as seven talks a day, a feat which would kill a lesser man, but which must account for the ease with which he exercises the clerical gift for bringing forth the sonorous familiar phrase of slowly deadening effect.

If parts of the biography also tend to anaesthetize, the reason may be that the book is one long encomium which nowhere questions the wisdom of any of the Cardinal's actions. This tends to make the reader feel that the portrait is one-dimensional and that a good man has been slighted by being given less weighty treatment than he deserves, but the subjects of biographies should properly be dead and the subject of this one is still very much alive. Fr. Gannon has had a difficult job and has done it with as much grace as could be expected.

Letter to Leo J. Zuber, undated

Sent three books back, kept 2 for pleasure & the rest for penance. You sure do get in a good penitential stock.

Mystics of Our Times

Hilda Graef. Hanover House, 1962.

The Bulletin, August 18, 1962

Mystics of Our Times contains ten short biographies of modern men and women who have lived the mystical life and concerned themselves with contemporary problems. The subjects, among which are both laymen and religious, are as diverse in temperament and interests as the American convert, Isaac Hecker, the Irish stenographer, Edel Quinn, and the French scientist, Pierre Teilhard de Chardin, S.J., but they all have in common that each was, in his way, ahead of his time, some by as much as a century. No stress is laid on mystical phenomena. The intention throughout has been to show that " . . . because our world is so distracting and, at the same time so desperately in need of God, He will give very special graces to those who, whether as priests or laymen, have been called to work for him in this world and who must use those means contemporary society has put at their disposal."

In spite of an undistinguished style, the book is enjoyable, easily read, and offers considerable food for reflection.

Letter to Leo J. Zuber, undated

I'll pass up Vol. 1 of the Newman biog. I am overloaded on Newman now.

Letter to Leo J. Zuber, September 23, 1962

I don't have a copy of that picture. I've looked and can't find anything. Listen, why don't you spare them my face? If you write FS&C, they can probably send you a picture of the jacket, *good advertisement and all. Tell them you want a picture of the jacket—barring that, they might have a picture of the picture I painted of myself but I would much prefer you use the jacket.*

A Sunday will be fine! Just let us know when.

Letter to Leo J. Zuber, October 1, 1962

This is such a short review maybe you could just put the initials at the bottom like they do at Jubilee. *I fixed it as usual but I think it looks silly with the byline.*

Thanks for the Reporter *with Bro. Antonius in it. I enjoyed it very much, and am going to pass it on to one of the Sisters at Rosary.*

What do you think of what the Archbishop has turned up with for editor of the Bulletin? *It all sounds good to me. I hope you manage to buttonhole Mr. G. Sherry* early on and get some of your ideas for the book page on his mind.*

If you could get them I would like "The Barbarian Within" by Walter Ong; Macmillan—and "Faith, Reason & the Gospels" by Heany; Newman.

P.S. Let us know what Sunday. We go in town to eat lunch but are always back by 2:30.

*Gerard E. Sherry, the new editor.

Letter to Leo J. Zuber, November 1, 1962

I think they're a little wacky at Jubilee *on principle. They certainly should have given the* Bulletin *credit for that review, the same as they gave it for the* Register. *The* Centurian. *If you direct your questions to Oona Sullivan, you will doubtless get a long letter.*

G. Sherry sounded a little like he was afraid you might have two heads. I hope he won't be too radical for the neighborhood. He probably thinks he's coming to the Bad Lands and has to be careful of everybody.

I hope all your sick are well again and that you all will be setting another date.

I owe you 5 reviews and I haven't forgotten. I've got to get this lecture trip over before I can think straight.

The Catholic in America

Peter J. Rahill. Franciscan Herald Press, 1961.

The Bulletin, November 24, 1962

The *Catholic in America* is a short history of anti-Catholicism in this country. Fr. Rahill confines himself to brief descriptions of the more obvious events that exemplify American anti-Catholicism and traces the gradual diminution of its vigor from Colonial times to the present. The book manages to be interesting in spite of the fact that it is written in a sloppy journalistic style (at one point the grammar is incorrect) and is not adequate to the complexity of the subject. No mention is made of that Catholic parochialism which often incited bitter feelings among non-Catholics. A good book can be written on anti-Catholicism in America but it would have to penetrate the subject to a greater depth than this one does.

Letter to Leo J. Zuber, December 1, 1962

This leaves me 3 to go which, they being all on St. V. de Paul, I'll do in one. I enjoyed reading about those Palomino rabbits. I didn't know there was any such beast.

When does old Gerard [Sherry] show up? I hope he won't be as businesslike as his letter—that will never go in the South.

Letter to Leo J. Zuber, December 21, 1962

This clears me up on the reviews and a good thing too since we don't know if old G. Sherry will want us around after the 1st of the year. Give me your impressions when you get a chance to have some.

reviews and letters

1963

Letter to Leo J. Zuber, January 6, 1963

Thanks for sending the Ecumenistr. *I'll write off for a free subscription. I have just seen the* Bulletin. *I was cheered not to see Joe Brieg the Rev. O'Brian and the teenage advice lady & to find Msgr. Conway in their places—a good balanced exchange. But where is theter book page? Where oh where?*

The Bible: Word of God in Words of Men

Jean Levie. Kenedy, 1962.

The Southern Cross, March 2, 1963

One of the most interesting facets of Church history in the last hundred years has been the strides made in Biblical scholarship. The purpose of this excellent book is to trace certain stages in the exegetical, archaeological and historical research of those years and thereby to show how the human aspect of Scripture appears today. The first half of the book is limited to the history of these new discoveries and the Church's response to them. The second part is designed to explore and emphasize the great complexity of Scriptural assertion. In it Fr. Levie discusses the various literary forms, the way sources are used and reproduced, the progressive character of the Old Testament and other related problems of historical exigency. Since the divine mes- [*line dropped in the printed review*] of its human author and since the individual exegete is not always able to determine between interpretations, it remains for the Church to judge its meaning. "God, who alone sees the ultimate connection between the doctrinal passages scattered throughout Scripture, gives to his Church, enlightened by the continual presence of the Spirit, the privilege of progressively gaining a deeper insight into the dogmatic synthesis he intended and willed from the beginning, and this as a result of the moral endeavors of the saints, the religious needs of the mass of the faithful, the scientific work of the exegetes, theologians and doctors, and the directives of the Magisterium." A knowledge of the material covered in this book should be part of the equipment of every Bible-reading Catholic.

Frontiers in American Catholicism

Walter J. Ong, S.J. Macmillan, 1957, 1961.

The Southern Cross, March 9, 1963

These six excellent essays, reissued here in paperback, are concerned with some of the cultural and ideological problems which face American Catholicism today. They are considered in the light of the American Catholic's attitude toward Europe and his own history, his misconceptions about the medieval period, and his attitude toward technology and science. They seem to be addressed as much to Europeans as to Americans. Fr. Ong believes that if Catholic thought in this country is going to have any real contact with the American experience it needs to envision "a real Christian mystique of technology and science." Ever since the bogus heresy of "Americanism"—ended by Leo XIII's letter to Cardinal Gibbons—Americans have been loth to explore the meaning of America for Catholicism. Fr. Ong believes that our intellectual contribution may be that of explaining the social surface of life in the United States—sports, luncheon, clubs, optimism, advertising, merchandising, etc.—along the lines of phenomenological analysis. He sees signs that there are some American Catholic philosophers who are becoming interested in phenomenology. These are fine essays and should not be missed now that they are available at this low price.

Letter to Leo J. Zuber, March 12, 1963

Thanks for the reviews. I'm cheered we ain't going to be extinct as reviewers but can continue on in ye olde So. Cross if that's the plan.

Mr. Sherry asked me for an article but for nothing else.

I hope you're getting over your illness. Every body around here has what is going around.

New Men for New Times

Beatrice Avalos. Sheed & Ward, 1962.

Seeds of Hope in the Modern World

Barry Ulanov. Kenedy, 1962.

The Southern Cross, March 16, 1963

Both of these books are concerned with new times, one with the education of the Christians who will live in them, the other with educating Christians to value them.

After two chapters analyzing the educational systems of

Marx and Dewey and their inadequate ways of meeting the uprootedness of modern man, Dr. Beatrice Avalos in *New Men for New Times* describes a Christian conception of education, the fundamentals of which she takes [to be] the principles and practices of a contemporary movement of Catholic action, the Schoenstatt Apostolic Movement. Her general thesis is that the sound exercise of activities on the natural level is the way to lay a solid foundation for the action of grace. She elucidates this in relation to person, home and school and provides the philosophical background. This book is written with intelligence and considerable learning but unfortunately with a heavy reliance, particularly in the first chapters, on the jargon held dear in educational circles. The rule is: if one word will do, use four; thus "experience" becomes "experiential contact with reality." Bastard words are either borrowed or invented, e.g., "educand"—an "educand" is presumably the victim of an educator. A boneyard of dead or abstract or unnecessary phrases is thrown up between the reader and the thought. If this were not a better book than most in this field, there would be no need to complain about this, but there is genuine danger that the reader, unless he is a student of education and thus habituated to such, will quit the book half way through, with the thought: if they do this to the language, what do they do to the child?

Dr. Ulanov's book, *Seeds of Hope in the Modern World*, should serve as an antidote to a tendency of Catholics to despise the modern world on principle and to condemn out of hand anything that does not have obvious roots in the Middle Ages. The author points out that "Meditation and contemplation in our time, like language and thought, do not often follow familiar paths. They could not, for the remarkable meditative minds of our time have looked elsewhere than to the familiar for their meditations. Or rather, they have looked through the familiar to the unfamiliar, have looked with such intensity and ingenuity and patience at the commonplace that they have discovered once again, as the Greek and Latin Fathers and the Renaissance humanists did before them, how very uncommon it is." Dr. Ulanov follows some of these meditations as they are found in modern literature, art, music and science. The procedure is much too rapid to be satisfying, but the book well achieves its purpose, which is to suggest the potential power of the modern world to lead a man closer to God.

The Wide World, My Parish

Yves Congar, O.P. Helicon, 1961.

The Southern Cross, March 23, 1963

Fr. Congar's book is concerned with eschatological questions and the meaning of salvation, particularly as it involves those outside the visible church. His intention is to provide "some elements" of answers to thoughtful people who ask questions about the salvation of "the others." This was a question which hardly occurred to the medieval mind, but which has grown in urgency as the world has been explored and other cultures discovered.

Understanding of the formula, "Outside the Church, no salvation," has changed drastically since the time of its originator, St. Cyprian, who understood it in an exclusive sense. Today it is understood to mean that the Church is the only institution to which universal salvation is committed, that she is the only institution able to ensure salvation for every person who does not refuse it.

There are equally good discussions here of the meaning of hell and the nature of purgatory and of the resurrection of the body. Altogether this is an admirable book. Significantly its title has been suggested by a quotation from John Wesley, "I look upon the world as my parish."

Letter to Leo J. Zuber, April 15, 1963

Cheered to get all the information. If somebody hasn't beat me to it, I'd like 63–27, the Weigel, and 62–158, the Foerster. If nobody wants the Zen dictionary before the Zen Catholicism *book comes, you can send me it with that and I can kill the two of them with one review.*

Cheers for The Southern Cross.

Letter to Fr. J. H. McCown, S.J., April 19, 1963

I enclose you the first issue of the new litry supplement of the new diocesan paper. The Archbishop has this new hot-headed crusader for editor now and the old paper is no more. He's a bit more of the crusader than most of us white scoundrels can take but anyway things are on the move in all directions at oncet and we endure it as best we can.

Letters from a Traveler

Pierre Teilhard de Chardin. Harper, 1962.

The Southern Cross, April 27, 1963

The American publishers of Père Teilhard de Chardin are probably waiting with interest to see what effect the recent Monitum issued by the Holy Office on his works will have on the sale of his books in this country. It is reasonable to suppose that it will have little appreciable effect, for the purpose of the warning is not to forbid the reading of Teilhard's books, but to point out to the reader what to beware of when he does read them. In any case, it should not affect the sale of *Letters to a Traveler* [*sic*], a collection of Teilhard's letters from China and Africa and America, written to his cousin, various colleagues and friends. The picture these letters give is one of exile, suffering and absolute loyalty to the Church on the part of a scientist whose life's effort was an attempt to fit his knowledge of evolution into the pattern of his faith in Christ. To do such a thing is the work of neither scientist nor theologian, but of poet and mystic. That Teilhard was to some degree these also is evident and that his failure was the failure of a great and saintly man is not to be questioned. The Monitum takes a most respectful tone toward the man himself, and these letters are further evidence that his life of faith and work can be emulated even though his books remain incomplete and dangerous.

St. Vincent de Paul

M. V. Woodgate. Newman, 1960.

The Holiness of Vincent de Paul

Jacques Delarue. Kenedy, 1960.

St. Vincent de Paul

von Matt and Cognet. Regnery, 1960.

The Bulletin, July 11, 1963

The three hundredth anniversary of the death of Vincent de Paul occurred in 1960 and these three volumes are a result of interest in the saint stimulated by that anniversary. The Woodgate book is a popular biography, adequate but not exciting in spite of the sharply dramatic life led by this shrewd peasant saint who grappled with the social ills of his day.

The Delarue book is better. It contains a short essay on the saint's life which traces his spiritual development from an ambitious young man to a devoted server of the poor. The rest of the book is made up of excerpts from St. Vincent's own letters, which is the proper place to find the spirit of the man.

The von Matt and Cognet book is perhaps the most satisfying of the three. It contains a short but very realistic life of the saint, interspersed with 190 magnificent photographs which have some connection with his time and place and the people who figured in his life.

These three volumes are a good beginning for anyone interested in the life of St. Vincent de Paul. It is a life which invites meditation and which no biography can exhaust.

Image of America

Norman Foerster. University of Notre Dame Press, 1962.

The Modern God

Gustave Weigel, S.J. Macmillan, 1963.

The Bulletin, September 26, 1963

These two books can be read together with considerable profit. Prof. Foerster's is a brief social and literary history of America from the Puritan Age through the deistic and romantic periods to the rise of realism and on to the present times of disillusion and search for something new worth believing in. Behind each of these changes in outlook is a different view of God and man's relation to him. The essays end in a brief consideration of the historical imagination as found in Southern literature, particularly Faulkner.

Prof. Foerster sees Americans as "an idealistic people, responsive to humanitarian impulses, believing in the dignity of man and the primacy of human rights, but confused, insecure, and anxious amid the forces of a world in turbulent revolution." Fr. Weigel begins at this point and analyzes the instability of the modern religious condition. He sees that our roots are in religious faith which we have not been able to throw off like the Russians but that in practical philosophy, we are as materialistic as they. Fr. Weigel discusses the place given God in the civic order, in the moral values of American culture, and by intellectuals. He ends by discussing the witness of the Church and its impression, or lack of impression, on the public conscience. He finds that our dilemma is too many weak secular faiths and suggests that what is needed is a "great faith resting on a big theology."

Both Prof. Foerster's and Fr. Weigel's are valuable essays which should add greatly to the Catholic's understanding of his country and his times.

Letter to Leo J. Zuber, September 27, 1963

Thanks for the offer of François Mauriac but I swear I am going to get through with these two I've got before I take on another.

That striped pony you sent us is an idea but I think we've got enough. You all had better come back soon. Marquita had her colt. He's black and his name is Equinox

O'Connor and I think your children should see him before he grows up and looks just like his pa.

Cheers. I will really try to send these two reviews before I am 70.

Evangelical Theology: An Introduction

Karl Barth. Holt, Rinehart & Winston, 1963.

The Southern Cross, October 24, 1963

Evangelical Theology: An Introduction contains the series of lectures Karl Barth delivered in the Spring of 1962 at the University of Chicago and Princeton Theological Seminary plus twelve additional chapters on the nature of the evangelical theologian's faith and work and the dangers which threaten them. Although the book is a description of his own beliefs about the subject, Barth does not use the term "evangelical" in the confessional sense. He points out that all Protestant theology is not evangelical whereas some Catholic and Eastern theology is. What the term designates is that theology which treats of the God of the Gospel. "Theology is science seeking the knowledge of the Word of God spoken in God's work—science learning in the school of Holy Scripture, which witnesses to the Word of God; science laboring in the quest for truth, which is inescapably required of the community that is called by the Word of God. In this way alone does theology fulfill its definition as the human logic of the divine Logos. In every other respect theology is really without support." Again, God "exercises law and justice when he makes the theologians, the church, and the world realize that even the best theology is in itself and, as such, a human work, sinful, imperfect, in fact corrupt and subject to the powers of destruction." This will remind the

Catholic of St. Thomas' dying vision of the Summa as all straw. There is little or nothing in this book that the Catholic cannot recognize as his own. In fact, Barth's description of the wonder, concern and commitment of the evangelical theologian could equally well be a description of the wonder, concern and commitment of the ideal Catholic life.

The Cardinal Stritch Story

Maria Buehrle. Bruce, 1959.

Leo XIII: A Light from Heaven

Br. William Kiefer, S.M. Bruce, 1961.

The Southern Cross, October 31, 1963

Here are two mediocre biographies of two great men. The biography of Cardinal Stritch, published only a year after his death, reads as if it were put together at high speed. A good biography of Cardinal Stritch or a memoir by someone who had been close to him would do much toward improving the popular image of the Catholic Church in this country, for he was one of the most distinguished, scholarly and charming of American churchmen. Miss Buehrle gives the facts and enough little anecdotes to make the Cardinal come through but the writing is tiresome and not what the subject deserves.

Brother Kiefer claims no more for his biography of Leo XIII than that it is adequate and the only one published in America since 1903. It does give a good and chilling picture of the condition of the Church when Leo became pope in 1878 and of the highlights of the troubles and accomplishments of the next twenty-five years. The persecution of the

Church in Italy at that time seems worse than her troubles in the Communist controlled countries today. This book will leave the reader looking for a more definitive treatment of its subject and perhaps that is as much as Brother Kiefer intended it to do.

What Is the Bible?

Henri Daniel-Rops. Guild, 1960.

Faith, Reason and the Gospels

Edited by John J. Heaney, S.J. Newman, 1962.

The Southern Cross, November 27, 1963

In these days of renewed interest among Catholics in the Bible and of considerable ferment in the field of Biblical criticism, it is essential that anyone interested in acquainting himself with Biblical literature, get started on the right foot. Henri Daniel-Rops' *What Is the Bible?* is an adequate short book for the beginner. It is a volume of the Twentieth Century Encyclopedia of Catholicism here reprinted in a hand-size 85¢ edition. It covers rapidly the history of the creation of the Bible, the times and places in which it was written and its authors. It is extremely simplified and should neither hold the student long nor satisfy his curiosity on the subject. Controversy is avoided.

Faith, Reason and the Gospels on the other hand is for the mature student who is perplexed by Biblical problems as they relate to scientific method. It is not designed for the nonbeliever but is meant to aid the man of belief to a better understanding of why he believes. Eleven of the articles included are by Catholics, four by Protestants. The collection grew out of and fulfills a distinct need. Although summaries of modern Christian thinking [in] regard to the gospels are available, they are for the most part confined to technical journals. This collection brings together in one volume such authorities in the field of Biblical studies as Fathers Jean Levie and David Stanley and Messrs. Floyd Filson and Archibald Hunter. It is a fine book, not easily exhausted.

Editor's note: This review also appeared in the *Catholic Week*, November 29, 1963.

Morte d'Urban

J. F. Powers. Doubleday, 1962.

The Southern Cross, November 27, 1963

Mr. Powers' novel, long awaited, has arrived and it is a fine novel, altogether better than the chapters published separately in the *New Yorker*, the *Critic*, and *Esquire* had led one to expect. These chapters were marked by a certain sameness that brooded [*sic*] no good for the future book, but the whole proves to be greater than the sum of its parts and moves forward without tedium to a profound conclusion.

The hero, Father Urban, is a go-getting priest in a non-go-getting order. His mission is to be the "better-type" soul and, against fearful odds, he manages to promote the construction of a golf course at his order's retreat house; but Father Urban's soul is worth saving and Mr. Powers proceeds to save it, even if ultimately at the expense of the golf course and the order's material gain.

In some circles this novel will be read as if it were an essay entitled "The Priest in America." Some reviewers will point out that Father Urban is not typical of the American priest; some will imply that he is. This reviewer would like to point out that Mr. Powers is a novelist; moreover a comic novelist, moreover the best one we have, and that Father Urban represents Father Urban. If you must look for anyone in him, Reader, look for yourself.

The Christian Opportunity

Denis de Rougemont. Holt, Rinehart & Winston, 1963.

Unpublished Review

In this collection of essays, Denis de Rougemont, the Swiss Protestant scholar best known in this country for the volume, *Love in the Western World,* analyzes the role the churches have played and should play to spread the Christian gospel in a secular middle-class world. He first examines the Nietzschean formula, God is dead (the gospel in reverse), and the Christian responses to it in a world where "our churches and the greater number of our faithful members have become . . . morality clubs rather than assemblies of pardoned sinners who, in prayer and worship, await the coming of the world without end." He believes that in this century when "the churches no longer find hostile doctrines in the world, but a doctrinal void that has no precedent," nothing will serve the Christian purpose but an uncompromising belief in transcendence and thus a transcendence involved in action. Instead the churches have been "feeble and absurd" and have compromised with the secular in everything from doctrine to decoration. He discusses the Christian opportunity in culture, in the family, in world problems and in ecumenism; his conclusions are realistic and on the side of optimism. De Rougemont knows more about Protestantism than he does about Catholicism but any Christian reader will find this book valuable.

Hear His Voice Today

J. Edgar Bruns, S.T.D. Kenedy, 1963.

Unpublished Review

In this introduction to the Bible the more important issues raised by each book of Old and New Testaments are briefly set forth together with an exposition of the principles of interpretation involved in them. The volume is intended primarily for the use of highschool and college students; its value will depend on how the student uses it. The exposition of each problem is too brief to be satisfying but the notes at the end of Part III may lead the student to other books which offer a more detailed treatment of the subject. Regarding the new Biblical studies, Fr. Bruns points out that Pius XII's encyclical, *Divino Afflante Spiritu*, appeared during the Second World War. "Those priests who were sent to study Sacred Scripture from this country could not have begun their courses at the Pontifical Biblical Institute in Rome or at the École Biblique in Jerusalem—the only existing authorized centers of Biblical studies for Catholics—before 1946. None of them would have been prepared to teach before 1948, and the first classes of Seminarians to benefit from their instructions could not have been ordained before 1953. It is, consequently, only a matter of ten years since any acquaintance with the trend in Biblical studies endorsed by the late Holy Father became general at all. There are still, undoubtedly, thousands of Catholics whose formal education was terminated by 1953 and who have merely been given to understand that there is a new approach to the Bible—often an understanding that is tinged with suspicion or hostility." Fr. Bruns' volume will help to bridge the gap.

Zen Catholicism

Dom Aelred Graham. Harcourt, Brace, 1963.

Zen Dictionary

Ernest Wood. Philosophical Library, 1962.

Unpublished Review

Zen is a form of meditation which has attracted considerable attention in the last few years in literary circles in America and with the wholesale consumption of Salinger on the campus, it has extended its attraction to students. Zen is neither a philosophy nor a theology, but a way of illumination which offers a definite release from the acquisitive values of American society. Much of its attraction can be accounted for by the fact that its attitude of enlightened non-attachment awakens the mind to the immediateness of our existence in God. Dom Aelred Graham believes that Zen has a definite message for the West but that this message will fail of its effect unless embodied in an existing Western tradition. " . . . the notion that Westerners can suddenly adopt a Japanese tradition, or that such a tradition may be transplanted to Europe and America without harm to Westerner values of great importance, argues considerable naivete." The purpose of Dom Aelred's book is to show that the fundamental intuitions of Zen are not unique, that they are in fact found in Catholicism to a marked degree. To enforce his points he cites not only the thought of mystics like St. John of the Cross and the author of *The Cloud of Unknowing*, but also to a considerable extent, St. Thomas Aquinas for whom Zen authors usually have a definite attraction. Dom Aelred has brought to attention a face of the Church which she seldom shows and which he believes she should begin to show if she is going to reveal herself truly to the modern world.

The *Zen Dictionary*, compiled by an authority on Oriental studies, covers all major aspects of Zen teaching and practice, Chinese as well as Japanese, and interprets Zen methods, the development of the Schools and life in the Zen monasteries. It is a handy reference book as well as good concomitant reading to *Zen Catholicism*.

reviews and letters

1964

Prince of Democracy: James Cardinal Gibbons

Arline Boucher and John Tehan. Hanover House, 1962.

The Southern Cross, January 9, 1964

Cardinal Gibbons' life was equivalent to a short history of the Catholic Church in America during its most crucial years. He lived from 1834 to 1921, saw the United States in three wars, and was an active churchman in the pontificates of four Popes, Pius IX, Leo XIII, Pius X—in whose election he played a decisive part—and Benedict XV. During these years in Europe the Church, shackled on every side by violently anti-clerical governments, was facing perhaps the blackest time in her entire history; only in America was she expanding. Cardinal Gibbons' great role was to recognize and proclaim to the rest of the Church what in America the separation of church and state had meant to the welfare of Catholics. His voice usually prevailed, not only in Europe but in this country as well, where Bishops were divided and charity among them was not conspicuous. He took a firm hand in molding the Church's position on labor, he effectively prevented the establishment of different national hierarchies in the United States, he founded the Catholic University in Washington and nursed it through many bad times, and he wrote the most popular book of apologetics of his age, *The Faith of Our Fathers*.

This biography by Arline Boucher and John Tehan is better written than most popular biographies and will whet the appetite for the definitive treatment of Cardinal Gibbons and his times.

The Kingdom of God

Edited by Louis J. Putz, C.S.C. Fides, 1962.

The Southern Cross, January 9, 1964

The Kingdom of God is an abridged Bible for school use, prepared for the German school system in 1960, and now available in English. There is no indication as to what grades this text is suitable for, but, since German schools are generally more advanced than ours, the German child would probably come to it several years before the American. The explanations before each reading are brief, stated in simple language, and designed to show the child what the ancient writer's intention was; for example, the explanation preceding Genesis I reads: "The Bible begins with a song of praise to God who created heaven and earth. God, through His Word, created and sanctified all things. The Bible gives its account of the creation of the world in the picture-story language of the ancients; consequently the work of creation is presented in the seven-day week framework." Old and New Testaments are tied in together with quotations in such a way as to assist the teacher to show the child that sacred history is a continuous revelation with the seeds of the future contained in the past.

It is doubtful if the illustrations in this text will appeal to children. In every face depicted, the sign for spirituality is emaciation. Otherwise, this is an admirable book, to be recommended for the child's use at home as well as in school.

Letter to Leo J. Zuber, April 5, 1964

Thanks for the note. I've been worried about having the Claudel book and not getting to it. I fell into the hands of the surgeons the last of Feb. and haven't been up to anything much since. Would you rather I sent the book back or kept it, waiting for a return of vigor? That will return slowly I am afraid.

I hope Blanch is okay and the children doing well.

author index

title index